The Searching Mind

The Searching Mind

An Introduction to a Philosophy of God

Joseph F. Donceel

UNIVERSITY OF NOTRE DAME PRESS

NOTRE DAME ~ LONDON

Copyright © 1979 by
University of Notre Dame Press
Notre Dame, Indiana 46556

9 8 7 6 5 4 3 2 1 0

Library of Congress Cataloging in Publication Data

Donceel, Joseph F   1906-
  The searching mind.

  Includes bibliographical references and index.
  1. God. I. Title.
BT102.D66   231   79-18166
ISBN 0-268-01700-X
ISBN 0-268-01701-8 pbk.

Manufactured in the United States of America

Contents

Preface

FIFTEEN YEARS AGO I published, with Sheed & Ward in New York, a small volume called *Natural Theology*. The title of the present, somewhat larger, book is more modest. It is an *introduction*. Not all the problems have been treated, and none of them has been treated exhaustively.

Despite its more modest title the present work is richer in content than the previous one. An effort has been made to show that the traditional First Way of St. Thomas Aquinas, a proof based on motion in the wide sense of reduction of potency to act, can really establish the existence of God. The demonstration based on the dynamism of the human intellect has been worked out in greater detail and with more accuracy. Kant's objections have been given more attention. A chapter has been devoted to the proof of God's existence presented by Maurice Blondel in his famous book *L' Action*. The second part, on the essence of God, has been even more thoroughly reworked. After a short study of the traditional doctrine, an attempt has been made to use some of the data of process philosophy and of the system of Hegel to develop a more acceptable doctrine of God's nature and to present a form of panentheism that might be defensible.

Yet the work remains an introduction to *a* philosophy of God. There are other ways of tackling the problem, of asking the questions and of trying to answer them.

It gives me great pleasure to express my gratitude to

Professor Piet Schoonenberg and to some of my former colleagues in the Philosophy Department of Fordham University: Professors W. Norris Clarke, Gerald A. McCool and Quentin Lauer, who have read my manuscript and offered valuable suggestions. They are, of course, not responsible for the shortcomings of the work.

Introduction

DESPITE THE MODESTY of the title of this book some readers may object to it. Their objection would run as follows: "You are writing an introduction to a philosophy of God. So you take for granted that God exists; you have no right to do so. Your main job is precisely to demonstrate that God does exist."

This point is well taken. It is a concrete way of stating a position that has often been advanced. Philosophy is a work of reflection. It hardly ever, if ever, discovers things of which we know absolutely nothing. It reflects on previously given experience. This experience is provided by life, not by philosophy, whose task is to examine and scrutinize it, to find whether and where it fits in the comprehensive conception of reality philosophy tries to elaborate.

Life provides most people with an idea of God. Even those who deny or doubt his existence have some, be it ever so vague, idea of what it is whose existence they are denying or calling into doubt.

Whoever examines human experience will eventually come across some special phenomena such as reverential awe, dread of the sacred, feeling of the mysterious and of the numinous, worship, religion. As one probes these undeniable data, he will quite naturally be led to examine whether the reality to which they seem to point does in fact exist and what kind of a being it is.

This might be a good way of starting toward a philosophy

1

of God. I have played with the idea of writing a book of this kind. I would have begun by summarizing Rudolf Otto's conception of the holy, tried to show that the feeling of the holy or of the numinous points to the existence of a transcendent reality, examined some other ways in which this same feeling has been interpreted by other thinkers (Feuerbach, Durkheim, Freud, Jung, Marx), compared and discussed these conflicting opinions. Thus we would have opened our study of God *via* the phenomenology of religion.

Of the reasons that have induced me to reject this possibility let me mention only the following one. Phenomenological studies are very difficult to summarize. It is precisely their wealth of details, the thoroughness with which all shades and nuances are set forth that makes them so valuable. A condensation does away with their very richness and robs them of their main value. It is better for the reader to study them by himself, either in the original works or in a good collection of readings. Therefore, I intend to restrict myself to the philosophical aspects of the investigation.

There is another way of tackling the problem: the historical approach. Why not briefly mention how, from its first faltering steps in ancient Greece, philosophy has always been interested in the divine, how the great philosophers tried to arrive at the existence and to study the nature of God? Such a historical approach is very fashionable nowadays, and it undeniably presents considerable advantages. Yet I shall not adopt this method either, for many reasons. First, such a historical survey will either be short and concise, and hardly do justice to the great philosophical systems of the past. Or it will require so much space and time that very little will be left for a systematic study of the problem. Moreover, what right do we have to restrict such a historical study to Western philosophy? Why not include a similar presentation of at least the Far Eastern thinkers with their rich and profound contributions? When would we ever get down to our main task?

Of course, even among philosophers who admit that God exists there are quite a number who are convinced that all efforts to establish the existence of God are doomed to failure. As philosophers they have settled for agnosticism with regard to God's existence. While they continue to admit God's existence for other than philosophical reasons, they are unwilling to try to make a case in reason for their conviction. So they may settle for a phenomenology of the religious feeling or a historical study of the various systems of natural theology.

I believe in the possibility of a philosophy of God, and I shall make an attempt to present in this book an elementary introduction into such a philosophy. I hold that the existence of God can be demonstrated, not in the strict sense of the word, in the way one may demonstrate a theorem in geometry, a law in science or a fact in history, but in the sense that we can make a case for it in reason, that we may vindicate our right of affirming the existence of God, that we may show that it is reasonable to affirm this existence, that we can discuss the problem intelligently, that we have an answer to the objections. It is true that our arguments cannot force the mind to assent; it can only invite it to do so, show that it is wise and prudent to do so. In the course of our vindication there comes a point where an option has to be made, where more than purely intellectual factors are at work. But this is true for all the important problems of philosophy: the existence of a spiritual soul, the freedom of the will, the meaning of life. If philosophy had to restrict itself to those topics where this is not the case, it would have to forego the study of all the basic problems of human life and of reality. This is what many contemporary philosophers do. They restrict their philosophical activity to a phenomenological description of human life, to an analysis of language or to a historical presentation of the great philosophical systems. They avoid the necessity of making an option, but their resolve to restrict themselves to "neutral" topics is itself the result of such an option.

Before I can start to present a philosophy of God a few important remarks have to be made.

1. Although I hold that God exists, I do not take for granted that my reader accepts this conviction. But I take for granted that he or she knows what we mean by the word 'God'. And to make sure that they do, I shall spell out as clearly as possible what meaning I attach to this term, so that we may speak of the same reality. In other words, we must start with a *nominal* definition of God.

Traditional philosophy made a useful distinction between two kinds of definition: real and nominal definition. A *real* definition is a statement which explains clearly and concisely what a being of our experience is. There is no doubt about the existence of such a being, for instance, of a cat or of a car. But we might like to have a definition of them, which explains clearly, for instance for purposes of taxation, how they differ, say, from a dog or from a boat. We are looking for a *real* definition of a cat or of a car.

We cannot start this work with a real definition of God, since we are supposed to find out whether or not such a being exists. Yet we must know what we are talking about; we must agree, for instance, that it is about God and not about gravitation that we are speaking. And therefore I have a right to start with a *nominal* definition of God, that is, one which does not presuppose or take for granted that he exists, but that sets down, as precisely and as concisely as possible, what we mean by the term 'God'.

In other words, personally I am convinced that God exists. I would like to tell my readers about the reasons I have for this conviction. But they and I have first to agree on what we mean by God. They may have a conception of God which I find unacceptable. Thus, unsophisticated readers might imagine God as an elderly, whitebearded king, whereas a sophisticated one may think of him as a finite and unconscious power. I shall certainly not try to show that such a God exists. It would not only be useless; it would also be impossible.

Therefore I feel entitled to state very precisely what kind of reality I mean by the God whose existence I shall endeavor to establish. Should somebody not accept my nominal definition, there is no point for such a person going any further with this book. I do not intend to make a case for the kind of God he has in mind, but only for the one I shall try to define nominally. Of course, my definition will not be arbitrary. The being I am defining in abstract philosophical terms is none other than the God of the judeo-christian tradition, the one about whom almost everybody in our Western world has heard.

So here is my nominal definition of God: the unlimited and necessary being. Let us briefly examine the three terms of this definition. God is a *being*,[1] in the sense of a reality, something that exists independently of my mind. He is *unlimited,* infinite, without any boundary, limit or restriction. This infinity is not extensive, spatial or quantitative, but intensive, ontic, in being. In simpler terms, God is not infinitely large or extended, but infinitely perfect, in all the senses of this word. He is *necessary.* If existing at all, he exists necessarily. God does not simply happen to exist, as we do, who might also not have existed. Not contingent, he is necessary.[2]

I expect some of my readers to accept without difficulty that God, if existing at all, is the unlimited, infinite being, but to object to my defining God as the necessary being. I wonder why. They cannot expect me to establish the existence of a contingent God, one who happens to exist, but who might as well not have existed at all. Such a God is not God for me, certainly not the God I shall try to make a case for in reason.

Somebody might say: Why not leave this controversial feature out of your definition? Why not simply state that you will demonstrate the existence of an infinitely perfect being, the creator of heaven and earth? Everybody would understand that definition, and nobody would be afraid that you might beg the question and trick him into admitting from the start that which you are supposed to demonstrate.

This objection allows me to try once more to clarify my position on this important aspect of our problem. The objection contains two parts, each of which I shall briefly discuss. First I am asked whether I cannot simply forego the element of "necessity" in my definition. I am not asked to establish the existence of a contingent God, but I am invited not to emphasize his noncontingent character. I reply that I need this element if I am to make a case at all for God's existence. It will become obvious, as we go along, why I cannot simply establish the existence of an infinitely perfect being if I am not allowed to take for granted that this being, if it exists at all, cannot not exist, is noncontingent, necessary. Moreover, it does not take much reflection to realize that "infinitely perfect" and "contingent" exclude each other. Of two beings, both supposed to be "infinitely perfect," one of which is contingent, while the other is necessary, there can be little doubt which is really infinitely perfect. The noncontingency is contained implicitly in the infinity. I mention it explicitly because I shall need it in my "demonstration," because I do not see how I can succeed in my endeavor if I am not allowed to make explicit use of it.

The second part of the objection alludes to the danger of "begging the question" if I start by defining God as the necessary being, the one who, if existing at all, exists necessarily. To this I reply that my definition is only a *nominal* definition. Strange as it may sound, the absolute necessity is only hypothetical. We are simply trying to agree what we are talking of when we speak of God. We are simply saying: let us agree that the being we have in mind is one who, IF it exists at all, cannot not exist, exists with absolute necessity, is necessary. This is the only God for whose existence I believe that I can make a case in reason. If I am not allowed to include this feature in my nominal definition, I must give up my attempt.

2. It is for the existence of an infinite and necessary being that I intend to make a case in reason. I do not say: It is the existence of such a being that I shall demonstrate. Let us be clear about this from the start. A demonstration is a proof in which the conclusion *follows* clearly from certain premises. What premises would we use in our present endeavor? The data of experience? All of them are finite and contingent. How can finite and contingent premises lead up to the existence of an infinite and necessary being? Philosophical principles? How can philosophical principles by themselves alone lead us to the *existence* of a real being? And what if these principles already implied the existence of God?

So I do not intend to "demonstrate" the existence of God. My purpose is more modest. My purpose is to make a "case in reason" for our affirmation of God's existence. What I hope to show is that the human person naturally affirms this existence and that the person has a right to do so. Of course, a steadily increasing number of people deny this existence. I would like to show that they continue to affirm implicitly what they deny explicitly, that there is a hidden contradiction, not in the statement by which they deny God's existence, but between the content of this statement and the *act* of stating it. What I purpose to do is to offer, not a demonstration of the existence of God, but a vindication of our right to affirm this existence.

3. Since the method that I shall use in this vindication is rather unusual, it will be useful if I gradually prepare my reader to the approach I intend to use. This approach is known as the *transcendental method*. Before giving a theoretical description of it, I shall show how it works in practice in connection with some of the features of the modern way of thinking which tend to turn many of our contemporaries away from admitting the existence of God. It is undeniable that the modern mind takes much less readily to an explicit and free acceptance of the

spontaneous affirmation of God than did the ancient and the medieval mind, or even the mind of the eighteenth and nineteenth centuries. The intellectual climate has so radically changed that what seemed fairly obvious in former times is much less so today.

In his book *Naming the Whirlwind: The Renewal of God-Language*[3] Professor Langdon Gilkey exposes four characteristics of the modern mentality which render it less open to the affirmation of God. People today are convinced of the contingency, the relativity, the temporality of everything in the world, and they are also deeply imbued with a sense of their own autonomy. Now each one of these traits makes it less easy for them to admit that God exists.

God has always been considered the necessary being who explains whatever is contingent. He is the Absolute, in whom nothing is relative. God is the eternal, without whom there would be no time, nothing temporal. Therefore, in traditional philosophy the contingency, the relativity and the temporality of the whole content of human experience pointed unmistakably toward God. The previous generations seemed unable to conceive of anything contingent that did not imply the existence of the necessary, of anything relative to which did not correspond some absolute reality, of anything temporal which did not refer to the eternal. It is a typical feature of the modern mentality that, for an increasing number of our contemporaries, this mental climate has totally changed. People nowadays are quite willing to admit that everything in their experience is contingent. It exists, but it might as well not exist. There is no real reason, no ultimate explanation, for its existence. We meet with explanations and logical connections only for the ordinary facts of daily life and within the scientific domain. But the important aspects of human life have no explanation and need none. Many have quietly taken in stride this basic unintelligibility of human life and of the universe.

As everything is contingent, so too everything is relative.

There are no absolute values, no absolute truths. What is valuable and true for me is not necessarily such for you. What is valuable and true today may no longer be such tomorrow, was not necessarily such yesterday. It follows that nothing is permanent, enduring; everything is in flux, changing, temporal. There is no eternal order of verities, of values; there is only the steady flux of ephemeral realities. When we are mindful that, if existing, God must be conceived as the necessary, the absolute and the eternal being who stands beyond the reach of all contingency, relativity and change, we realize how poorly disposed the modern mind is for admitting the existence of God.

The first three features mentioned by Professor Gilkey cast a rather gloomy pall over life. Not so the last one to which he refers. Our contemporaries attach great importance to the autonomy of man.[4] He is the master of his own fate; he sets his own goals; he creates his own values. Nobody can dictate to him or impose his will upon him. Man is a free and sovereign being. It is easy to see that this deep conviction of modern man will not induce him easily to accept the existence of a sovereign Being on whom he totally depends, to whom he owes total allegiance.

It looks, therefore, as if the task of establishing the existence of God in the face of so deep an opposition is well nigh impossible. Yet there are some good reasons for not giving up right away. In the last part of his book Gilkey points out that twentieth-century man does not seem to be all that certain of these highly touted convictions. If you stop listening for awhile to what he loudly proclaims and watch him in his daily life, especially in the more dramatic or unsettled moments of this life, in periods of stress or exaltation, when he shakes off the daily, dulling routine and faces the unusual, the novel, the primordial, the fundamental, at times of birth, marriage, pain, misfortune, loneliness, illness and death, the picture changes considerably. The way he reacts in these moments, the way he lives them, does not seem to agree with the way he speaks at duller moments. There is, says Gilkey, an element of ultimacy, of transcendence, which occasionally crops up in almost every human life and which cannot be reconciled with the philosophy mentioned above.

Be that as it may, I am interested in another aspect of the modern mind as described above. There is something strange in it which makes some of its claims sound rather questionable. It looks very much as if man held *absolutely* that there are no absolutes, that everything is relative. For him the contingency of whatever exists seems to be a *necessary* feature of every reality. He speaks as if the temporality and transitoriness of everything in this world were an *eternally* true aspect of it. There seem to be contradictions in these positions.

Let me make this clearer by concentrating on a couple of them. Great emphasis is placed nowadays on such claims as that every truth is relative, historical, time-conditioned. This means that it is true here and now, but that this does not necessarily imply that the same affirmation will also be true at a later time, in other circumstances. However, does the one who claims that all statements are time-conditioned not unconsciously make an exception for this, his own affirmation, by which he claims that the truth of all affirmations is time-conditioned? If he does, he claims implicitly that this, his own affirmation, is always true, at all times, in all places, therefore that it is not time-conditioned. He contradicts himself, not explicitly, but implicitly. This means that although there is no contradiction in his statement, there is one between the statement and the act by which it is affirmed. What one might claim without any danger of contradiction is that *almost all* truths are time-conditioned. I would easily go along with that, since it admits of exceptions, be they ever so few. It is precisely in these few exceptions that I am interested, because it is among them that we shall find the affirmation of the existence of God.

Or take another fashionable assertion: All statements are

true only within a certain framework. If this is taken once more as applying to *almost all* statements, there is no objection. But if it is really meant universally, it seems to me to contain an implicit contradiction. It claims that all statements are true only within a certain framework, within a certain linguistic, social or historical context. Now this is a statement. It is true only within a certain framework; it is not always true; it does not apply to absolutely all affirmations, always and everywhere. In some other framework it might not be true. How then can anybody without implicit contradiction claim that all statements are true only within a certain framework? Here again this position can be held without implicit contradiction only by allowing for exceptions. It is my claim that the affirmation by which we assert that God exists belongs among these exceptions. For it is a metaphysical affirmation, and metaphysics is the framework of all frameworks: it is the universal framework.

What I have done here against the agnostic position of many contemporaries is to use what is sometimes called *retortion*. It consists in this: we point out that someone who denies a certain truth affirms it implicitly in the very act by which he denies it. The *content* of his denial tries to invalidate a position which the very act of denying upholds. This manner of arguing is offensive to many good minds. They consider it unfair. At first sight it may indeed look unfair, since it tries to establish a position against an opponent's denial by humiliating the opponent, by pointing out that he contradicts himself, that he offends against the most elementary rules of logic, that he does not know how to argue intelligently. Even if what he says contained an implicit contradiction, would it not be more courteous to overlook it and to try to demonstrate one's own position in some other, less offensive, way?

The trouble is that there is no other way in which such positions can be vindicated. What my interlocutor denies is what I consider one of the basic truths of metaphysics, or, to put it less technically, one of the fundamental certitudes of human life. Now, if it is a *fundamental* certitude, all other certitudes are ultimately based upon it, and it is not itself based on any other. How then am I to make a case for it should somebody reject it? My only way is to try to show that every human mind holds this truth, that holding it goes together with having a human mind, that it is simply impossible to deny it. How am I to establish this against those who stoutly deny that they hold this truth? There seems to be no other way than to ask these people whether they hold it and, should they claim that they do not, to show them (as courteously as possible) that, in fact, they do implicitly affirm it in their very denial. That is precisely what retortion is all about. It may appear to be a rude and discourteous manner of doing the job. Unfortunately it is also the only manner of doing it.

Retortion was used by Plato, Aristotle and Aquinas. It continues to be used, under this or some other name, by many contemporary thinkers, philosophers and others. Thus the famous sociologist Peter L. Berger used it a few years ago when he wrote: "One (perhaps literally) redeeming feature of sociological perspective is that relativizing analysis, in being pushed to its final consequence, bends back upon itself. The relativizers are relativized, the debunkers are debunked, indeed, relativization itself is somehow liquidated."[5]

Some people get the impression that retortion is merely a semantic trick, a playing with words. They maintain that you cannot establish a basic certitude by using a few words. The strange thing, however, is that they try to invalidate it in exactly the same way, by means of a few words! The fact is that we have to do here with much more than a few words, with acts of the mind, with affirmations. What retortion tries to show is that whenever man uses his mind, he unconsciously and necessarily affirms certain things. Using his mind, thinking, making these affirmations always go together. It follows that the only way in which a person can refrain from making these affirmations is by not using his mind, by not thinking or talking. Such a person is irrefutable. We do not discuss with him. He is, said Aristotle, like a tree stump. But whoever denies these basic certitudes runs the risk of being shown up as asserting implicitly what he denies explicitly.

The reason why I insist at such length on these considerations is that, better than anything else I could do, they shed light on the very peculiar nature of the affirmation of God's existence and of my attempt to make a case in reason for its truth. As I mentioned above, this affirmation cannot be demonstrated in the strict sense of the word. Its truth cannot be deduced from a study of the facts or from a collection of abstract principles. It looks more and more as if the only way of establishing it is some kind of retortion.[6]

I make bold to say that every human mind, necessarily although unconsciously, affirms the existence of God in every one of its existential affirmations. By the latter expression I mean every affirmation which asserts that something exists, which puts us in contact with some reality. The affirmation of God is part of the set of basic certitudes which are given to human beings together with their mind. This set of basic certitudes has been traditionally known as *metaphysics*. The whole set of them is globally asserted every time man uses his mind, whenever he thinks or speaks or acts in a human way. So it is impossible strictly to demonstrate any one of them, since each one will be used in the very demonstration. But each one will also be used in the act by which somebody might deny them.

4. The transcendental method in philosophy, which I shall use in my undertaking, studies the conditions of the possibility of any act of intellectual knowledge. It is obvious that in order for persons to think, certain conditions must be fulfilled. If and when they think, they implicitly affirm that these conditions are fulfilled. There are some very obvious conditions: they must have a mind, their memory must be reliable, they must be

capable of understanding and using a language. Suppose that a hypercritical doubter—such people exist—would tell me: You take for granted that you remember the exact meaning of the words you use. You trust your memory. What right do you have to do so? I would answer: "I have as much right to do so as you. You trust not only your memory, you trust mine too! You take for granted that the words you use in this, your objection, really mean what you think they mean. You also take for granted that I understand them (at least roughly) in the same sense in which you do! You cannot say that you do not rely on your memory without relying on it!"

It is obvious that we cannot think or know unless we have a mind, unless we trust our memory and are capable of using a language. There is more, however. Thinking is an activity. When we think, we are not passive; we are active. If thinking is an activity, we contribute something to it: there is something which comes from us in everything we think or know. This contribution from our own minds in whatever we think or know is an a priori condition of the possibility of all thinking and knowing. It can be shown that this contribution consists in the affirmation of the basic certitudes of life, of what is traditionally known as the great principles of metaphysics.

I cannot spend much time demonstrating this here. Let me briefly mention one argument. If you admit that as a being is, so it acts, and also that the human person has a soul and a body, it follows that this person's thinking too, since they are his activities, are composed of two elements which stand to each other somewhat as the soul stands to the body. The soul of our thinking and knowing consists precisely in metaphysics, that is, the basic certitudes of life. It follows that metaphysical statements cannot be really demonstrated. To demonstrate implies to think. To think implies to assert and to use the basic metaphysical principles. Thus we would be able to demonstrate them only by taking them for granted. We may establish or vindicate these affirmations only by challenging all comers to deny them and showing that they too affirm them in their very denial. I hold and I shall try to show that the affirmation of God's existence is one of these basic affirmations which cannot be really demonstrated, which we affirm whenever we think or know, which cannot be denied without an implicit contradiction.

5. For many people all of this amounts to a very unsatisfactory state of affairs.

a) This is especially true for people who, in the discovery of knowledge, like to proceed in an orderly and methodical way. They would like to start from an obvious fact or experience and gradually arrive at solid conclusions based on them. Nothing of the kind is possible here. There is no real starting point; there is no conclusion. Or rather the starting point is the same as the conclusion. The only transition which occurs in the present case is that from the implicit to the explicit, from the unthematic to the thematic. My claim is that every human being affirms that God exists. But one does so unconsciously, unthematically, implicitly. One *lives* this affirmation; we might say that one IS such an affirmation, that the human person is an embodied affirmation of the Necessary Infinite Being. But very frequently one is not aware of it. My purpose is to render everyone aware of it.

b) The situation is also unsatisfactory in another respect. What comes first: metaphysics or natural theology? With what must we start, with the study of being or with the study of God? From what has been said above it is clear that we cannot start with either of them without also taking up the other. In this respect metaphysics (including the philosophy of God) differs considerably from most other sciences. Studying metaphysics is like building an arch, while studying the sciences looks more like building a wall. In building a wall, at least in the old-fashioned way of the stone masons, you simply put one layer of bricks upon the other. You would never dream of skipping a layer here and there, or of starting with the top of the wall. So too in the study of science: you start with the beginning and keep using what has been established in order to make further progress. The procedure is orderly and acceptable to the human mind. Not so when you build an arch. You cannot simply start with the lower bricks and gradually build higher on them. The structure will collapse. The bricks of the arch proper are held in place not only by the ones under them but also by the ones above them. The ideal way of building would be to set all the parts of the structure down at once. Since this is not possible, a wooden framework is required, upon which the bricks may be put. It does not matter too much now where one starts, since the arch will hold only when the last brick is in.

So it goes with metaphysics. Every part of it supports the others and is supported by them. Every truth in it supposes the others and is supposed by them. There is a "circumincession" of all metaphysical principles. Hegel insists frequently on the circular nature of what he calls the science of logic. Metaphysics would be obvious and without need of proof or explanation if it were possible to present all its verities in one fell swoop. Since this is excluded, any attempt at demonstrating a truth in metaphysics will look, to the attentive student, like some kind of *petitio principii,* like a begging of the question. Since the solidity of metaphysics consists in its self-supporting unity, every effort made to analyze it will weaken it. It is no wonder, then, that analytical philosophers are puzzled by it and reject it out of hand. This does not mean that we are not supposed to examine it, to take it apart, to analyze it. How else are we to study it? But such an analysis will create false and insoluble problems which can be solved only if the analysis always takes place against the background of a comprehensive synthesis.

So we may start with the study of being and also with the study of God. There is no real starting point, as in a circle. Our procedure will necessarily be artificial. Somewhat as with our first attempts at swimming: we can learn the swimming motions only in the water. Yet before having mastered these motions, we should not jump into the water. In spite of this theoretical impossibility we managed to learn to swim, although our first attempts were far from elegant.

c) There is another aspect of this problem which is disagreeable to many minds. Our enterprise is basically a metaphysical one. Now, as was argued above, we never offer a real "demonstration" or "proof" in metaphysics. So the reader will never be able to perceive, to see that what I say is true. And yet, if one follows me, one may have to admit that it is. What one sees is this: if one admits the starting point, one *cannot not affirm* the conclusion.

This seems to contradict what was said above about there being no real starting point. True, but remember I explained that, on account of this very fact, my procedure will have to be artificial. There is a starting point of sorts, but it already contains implicitly the final conclusion. I must start somewhere. I cannot dump the argument wholesale into the reader's lap. I shall use as a starting point something which everybody will readily admit without being aware of all that this admission implies.

All of this points to one more essential feature of metaphysical thinking. We have no intuition of the basic certitudes of life.[7] We do not *see* them; we have to affirm them. Our substitute for the missing intuition is "unavoidable affirmation." Sartre has made the profound remark that the human being is doomed to freedom. One is free, but one is not free to be free. One cannot help being free. Something similar occurs in the line of thinking. We are doomed to affirm the basic certitudes of life, the fundamental principles of metaphysics. We affirm them necessarily. True, some people deny them. But only explicitly, not implicitly. Implicitly they continue to affirm them, even in their very act of denial, as *retortion* points out.

Such is the way in which we know of the existence of God. We do not *see* that he exists; we have no intuition of him. But we cannot not, at least implicitly, affirm his existence.

6. What we have said above may explain to some extent something which puzzles those who advert to it. The human mind spontaneously admits the existence of God, or, to put it more vaguely, the reality of the Divine. It seems therefore that this truth should be not only obvious but also very easy to establish. Yet we notice that those who endeavor to establish it hardly ever agree on the best way of doing it. They demolish each other's arguments and come forward with their own way of proving the truth of God's existence. The thing is obvious as long as you do not try to establish it, to analyze it. We may now understand why this fundamental truth of human existence is at the same time so evident (that is why the majority of unsophisticated minds accept it at once) and so difficult to demonstrate or to establish in reason. Just as the beauty of a musical score or of a poem vanishes under analysis, so the evidence of this truth disappears when you start analyzing it. Analyzing a score or a poem is enriching only if it is done to make possible a richer synthesis. Making a case in reason for the existence of God makes sense only if it helps us to become aware of what we have always already known.

Simple people do not analyze much, and for most of them God's existence is obvious. Among the sophisticated some analyze too much, without being aware that analysis must be backed up by synthesis. This is especially true of thinkers whose bent is for scientific work and for philosophers with a positivistic or analytic turn of mind. For them the obvious ceases to be obvious. Some of them may continue to hold that God exists, but they claim that his existence is known only through belief or faith.

7. To me this sounds like an unacceptable abdication of human reason, like intellectual defeatism. It means that it is not

reasonable, wise and prudent to affirm God's existence. When something is reasonable, wise and prudent, one should be able to give reasons for it. According to this fideist position, belief in God may be traditional, comforting, useful, fashionable; it may provide us with a sense of security and fill a gap in our heart. But it cannot stand the test of rational scrutiny: it is a point which you cannot intelligently discuss, any more than you discuss a person's culinary or esthetic preferences. *De gustibus et coloribus non disputatur*.

When somebody claims that admitting the existence of God is a matter of belief or of faith, what does one mean by belief or faith? Is it the child's spontaneous belief in his educators, in what some psychologists have called the "prestigious authorities" of the early years? Or does one mean religious faith, that which some christians know as the theological virtue of faith?

It is difficult to admit that this is simply a case of natural belief. There are so many things which we believed as children (the stork, Santa Claus, the existence of Australia). Some of these beliefs have been given up, because we never came across any evidence for them. Others have been retained, because they were strengthened by new evidence or testimony. Why did many of us keep our belief in God? Is it not because we have met new evidence for it? And is this evidence not the fact that we found it reasonable to admit God's existence? It is true that most of us *started* to believe in God because, when we were young, our parents told us about him. But the reason why most of us continue to admit his existence is no longer the word of our parents. Something else has taken over in our mind. What is this something else?

Some christians say that it is what theology calls the supernatural virtue of faith, infused at baptism and starting to operate on the level of consciousness with the awakening of the mind. This faith has undoubtedly been a major influence upon many a person's conviction that God exists; it explains why this conviction becomes virtually unshakable. But to admit that it is the *sole* reason for it brings up considerable difficulties. Supernatural faith consists in believing something because God himself has revealed it, has told us that it is true. In this hypothesis we would be convinced that God exists because he himself has told us so. This might be unobjectionable if we were able to meet God the way we may meet a human being. When somebody tells us that he or she is John Doe or Mary Roe, we act reasonably in admitting this. But the case is quite different with God. We are supposed to know *nothing* about him from reason or from experience; what we hear about him from others is said *never* to receive any experimental or rational confirmation. Firmly to believe that he exists because he himself—the utterly unknown—tells us that he does seems to be a case not of faith but of gullibility.

Rather, what seems to happen is that before welcoming God's revelation, we somehow know that and what he is. "Before" implies, not any chronological, but only a logical and ontological, priority. As children we believed God's existence somewhat as we may have believed that of the stork or of Santa. But there is a great difference between these two kinds of belief. The latter have no roots in our mind; soon they wither and die. The former is deeply rooted in our intellect; most people welcome it, a few of them after having critically examined it. Although it never becomes overwhelmingly clear, it can withstand difficulties, doubts and denials. This is not the effect of the sole virtue of faith. As Professor L. Malevez put it,

> The act of faith refers definitely to an Absolute who is implicitly affirmed by our intellect. When we state, in the act of faith: it is God who speaks in Jesus Christ, we refer this word to the Absolute who is already written in our mind, we claim that it possesses the features of a God whose existence we naturally affirm . . . . It is on account of this relation to the implicitly affirmed God that the God of revelation and of faith assumes a meaning *for us* and becomes *our* truth. In other words: it is

> impossible to believe in revealed theology without the "exercise" of a natural theology. This natural theology does not have to be explicit . . . . But it must have been "lived" implicitly by our reason. Otherwise the affirmation of the God of revelation would make no sense for us.[8]

8. Strongly as I reject fideism and agnosticism in connection with the existence of God, I readily admit that what reason tells us about him is vague, hazy and far from satisfying to our mind's craving for clear knowledge. We have already mentioned one reason for this state of affairs: we do not *see* that God exists and what he is. Yet we cannot not affirm the existence of a being about which we realize at once that we cannot really fully grasp it.

It is undeniable that, were it not for revelation, we would know very little about this Absolute whose existence we necessarily affirm. The case of the two philosophical giants of antiquity is most instructive in this respect. Although, for the reasons mentioned above, I do not intend to devote much space to historical notes, an exception must be made for them. It seems certain that they have not been affected by Old Testament revelation, and they wrote several centuries before the christian era. Their work exemplifies what we said above: from reason alone we know about the existence of God, but what we know about him is not much and not clear.[9]

Plato (427–347 B.C.) believed in a plurality of gods that had some resemblance with the gods of traditional greek religion but differed from them because they loved the truth and lived moral lives. For him the greatest of the gods was the world as a whole. About this supreme god he writes in the last sentence of his *Timaeus* (92c):

> and here we may say our discourse of the universe has at last come to its end. For with this our world has received its full complement of living creatures, mortal and immortal, and come to be in all its grandeur, goodness, beauty and perfection, this

visible living creature made in the likeness of the intelligible and embracing all the visible, this God displayed to sense, this our heaven, one and only-begotten.

This world has a soul which possesses in a preeminent way the character of divinity. Plato attributed the formation of the world to what he called the *Demiurge*, who seems to.be nothing but a "mythical projection of the world-soul." Plato speaks at times as if the highest Idea, that of the Good, were his God. The Idea of the Good is for him the most perfect reality, and, in this sense, it might be considered God. Yet he never calls it that, but he refers to it as divine, as the divine. If Plato's God is a personal being, it is difficult to see how the Idea of the Good can be God. An obvious solution of the difficulty is to put the ideas, including that of the Good, in the World-Soul and thus to harmonize the two strands of Plato's theology. Yet this solution, which has been adopted by many of his followers, seems never to have occurred to Plato himself.

For *Aristotle* (384–322 B.C.) God is the *Pure Act* that explains every motion in the world. "The activity exercised by the pure Act cannot be physical. Therefore it must be a conscious activity. It will consist of a knowledge without successivity or discursivity, in a purely mental contemplation. This highest act of knowledge must have the highest and most perfect object, which can be no other than the essence of God itself. Therefore God is self-contemplating contemplation."[10]

This Pure Act has not made the world, which exists from all eternity. It is the cause of all movement within it: not, however, its efficient cause, but its final cause, its aim or end. If God were the efficient cause of movement, the fact of producing it would introduce a change in him, which would detract from his immutability. Aristotle's God moves the world as that toward which the world strives, that which it loves. He is loved by all things, but he himself does not love them nor does he direct the world through any providence.

This short summary of the philosophical theology of the two greatest prechristian thinkers of our Western world shows two things: 1) that unaided human reason can reach God and 2) that it does so in a vague and hazy way. Thinkers influenced by the judeo-christian revelation consider some aspects of this philosophy of God deficient. For Plato God seems to be the World-Soul, and a purely immanent World-Soul. This has the great advantage of explaining how God causes and directs all that happens in the world; it admirably explains his immanence in the world. But his transcendence seems to be seriously endangered. If God is the immanent soul of the world, he stands on its level; he is not infinitely beyond it, he is not transcendent. Aristotle safeguards God's transcendence. But he seems to do so at the expense of his immanence. A God who neither knows nor loves nor directs the world differs certainly from our usual conception of him.

Since we are committed to try to investigate the problem of God through reason alone, as Plato and Aristotle did long ago, we shall meet the same problems which confronted them.

9. We seem to know much more, and that more clearly, about God nowadays than Plato and Aristotle did. Does this progress in our knowledge derive from philosophy? Does it not come from revelation and from theology? It is difficult to deny that revelation and theology have influenced our knowledge of God. To what extent? And does this not once more bring up the question whether, by his unaided reason, a human being is capable of establishing the existence of God?

All the great philosophers of the West who wrote within the christian era, with the possible exception of Plotinus (third century A.D.), have been directly or indirectly influenced by christianity, hence by revelation. This is not true of the great thinkers of the Far East. But their philosophy is generally a mixture of philosophy and religion. And they are far from agreeing about the nature of the Absolute.

There are philosophers in the West who have tried to shake off all the christian influences. Most of them also deny the existence of God or claim that reason cannot establish it. It looks very much as if a philosophy of God of the kind which I am trying to present in this work is possible only within an attitude of faith. I am more and more willing to admit the position of Professor Henri Bouillard when he writes that natural theology is "the rational *intrastructure,* and not strictly speaking the infrastructure of christian theology."[11] To consider natural theology the rational *intra*structure of christian theology is to claim that it makes real sense only within an attitude of faith. Not only does it render this faith reasonable, as explained above, but it also derives much of its own solidity from this faith itself. Faith and christian theology have an influence upon the philosophy of God, making it clearer, more sure of itself. What natural theology provides is a rather vague outline of the conception of the necessary and infinite being. It is quite sure that such a being exists; it shows us clearly that to deny this entails a lived contradiction. But this undeniable being is infinitely remote from us. Left to our own devices, we can only have a hazy idea of it. But what we thus dimly catch sight of fits in very well with the much clearer and more distinct notion of God provided by faith and christian theology and receives a remarkable confirmation from them.

A *mortise,* says the dictionary, is a notch, hole or space cut in a piece of wood to receive a corresponding projecting piece called a *tenon,* formed in another piece of wood, in order to fix the two together.

The main conclusion of natural theology, that there really exists a necessary and infinite being, looks like a tenon. It makes full sense only within its mortise. In our case the mortise is faith. Faith needs the tenon of natural theology. Lacking it, what faith has to tell me would be of no interest to me. It would be like a lump of gold in my stomach. My stomach does not care for gold, however precious it may be. A mind without an at least "exercised" natural theology would not be interested in listening to God's revelation, would not even understand what the term 'God' means.

The interaction is reciprocal. In the light of faith the conclusion of the philosophy of God turns from hazy to clear, from shaky to firm. Let me use another comparison to illustrate this important point. Modern archaeologists have received a great boost in their work from aviation. They might be examining a promising site, where they have good reasons for believing that ancient ruins are hidden. As long as they walk around on the ground while they probe for the ancient structures, they may discover nothing. But once they are airborne and flying over it, the great lines of the buried constructions become unmistakable. Somewhat in the same way the height which we reach through faith may make clearer to us the path our mind is to travel to reach, *by its own means,* the firm conclusion that God exists.[12]

It is therefore in this spirit that the present work is offered to the reader: in a spirit of sincere respect for agnostics and atheists. The claim that they remain unconvinced by my arguments is understandable. They cannot possibly force the assent of one's mind. They receive their *full* value only *from the light toward which they point, without containing it in themselves.* I feel unable to make atheists or agnostics discover a God whom they do not yet yearn for in the depth of their heart, or, rather, *the unconscious yearning for whom they do not explicitly admit.* This book is written not so much for them, but rather for believers, to whom it wishes to show that they are right in admitting the existence of God, that this is a reasonable thing to do, that it lies in the prolongation not only of the innermost yearning of the human heart but also of the undeniable upward surge of the intellect and the will. It may help them answer the objections of the atheist and show the latter that the theist is able to marshal reasons which are not shallow and deserve to be respected and carefully examined.

Since the philosophy of God makes full sense only within an attitude of faith, as the latter's intrastructure, I shall feel free, in this work, to listen at times to what faith and theology can tell me and to examine my own findings in the light which they may shed. I shall, of course, have to be very careful not to use these nonphilosophical data in my philosophical thinking itself. I intend to respect the autonomy of philosophy. The advantages deriving from such occasional incursions into theology are so considerable (especially for the kind of readers I envisage for this book) that they warrant running the risk of turning away other potential readers. To the nonbelievers whom this christian kind of philosophizing would not right away deter I would suggest that they might consider my theological speculations as mere hypotheses that may help us find our way more easily in the philosophical tangle. The precedent of such illustrious philosophers as Hegel and Blondel (not to speak of the great medievals) shows clearly that this procedure is not unheard of in philosophy.

10. Before setting out on my own task, I shall briefly state my position in a question which comes up in connection with the term 'God'. Is it a proper name which means nothing but only designates a certain individual, such as Paul or Mary? Or does the term have a meaning which describes a certain function such as pope or king, without referring directly to any individual? It looks as if the term 'God' may be used in both these capacities. In prayer people use the word as a name by which they address the divinity. Yet the name obviously has a meaning. For our purpose it means "the infinitely perfect and necessary being." Despite what some philosophers claim, it does not seem that one sense necessarily excludes the other. There are other instances in our language where the same term may mean one individual person and also a certain function, as in the case

where we address somebody as 'Bishop' or 'Governor'. I submit therefore that the term 'God' functions primarily as a description in the sense mentioned above. But since such a being is, of its very nature, unique, it is also often used as a proper name.[13]

The Existence Of God

DESPITE THE DIFFICULTIES mentioned above, I must, in order to present my views with a maximum of clarity, arrange them in a certain order. That is why my work will, somewhat artificially, be divided into two parts, the first of which will try to show *that* God exists, while the second part will investigate *what* or *who* God is. The reader realizes, and I wish to emphasize once more, how artificial such a procedure is. How can I show *that* God is unless I know first *what* he is? So there unavoidably will be a considerable amount of overlapping. I shall try to keep it to a minimum, and although, as the reader has been warned, the study of metaphysics, hence also of natural theology, is "circular," I shall see to it that the circle in question is not a vicious one.

We can demonstrate that something exists either directly from experience or indirectly through reasoning from something we know from experience. Thus I know that Paris exists, because I have been there. We do not know God directly from experience. A few individuals, in every place and time, have claimed that they know him in this way. They are called "mystics," and their experience is known as "mystical experience." Although the danger of delusion is very great in this domain, it is undeniable that there have been—and that there still may be—authentic mystics who have really had an experiential knowledge of God. I further believe that rudimentary mystical experiences do not occur as unfrequently as some people would believe. I am thinking of cases where a person may, amidst favorable circumstances (a lonely walk in the woods or along the shore, under a starry sky; or an impressive religious ceremony in a setting of great beauty and devotion), but also at times quite unexpectedly, in the most unlikely setup (for instance, waking up from an afternoon nap), suddenly get an overwhelming, awe-inspiring, crushing impression of the presence of a sacred mystery that is everything and in whose presence one feels like nothing.[1] That such experiences do occur with a certain frequency seems to be certain. Whether they are really mystical experiences is debatable. At any rate, neither such rudimentary experiences nor even the high mystical encounters of authentic mystics with the Absolute can be used in a "demonstration of God's existence," because all of them fall within the private domain and remain, of their very nature, purely personal and incommunicable.

Since we cannot establish the existence of God directly from experience, we must proceed indirectly. Pure reasoning will not do; we must start from a fact, from an undeniable fact of experience. Reasoning from experience may be a posteriori or a priori. It is *a posteriori* when that which serves as the starting point of the argument is posterior to that which must be established, when it comes after it, follows from it, sometimes in time, always in nature. This kind of reasoning generally proceeds from the effects to the cause. Thus: the lawn is drenched; it must have rained. The following symptoms are present; this person has pneumonia. Reasoning is *a priori* when that which serves as its starting point is prior to the fact or state of affairs which is to be established. Here we generally pass from the cause to the effect. Thus: it has rained throughout the night; the lawn must be drenched. Tom has pneumonia; therefore he breathes with difficulty.

It is obvious at once that God's existence cannot be established a priori, since nothing can be prior to God, since he has no cause. Therefore we shall have to try to reach him a posteriori, by considering some of the effects of his activity.

There is another kind of reasoning that is sometimes called a priori, although it is not strictly such. Nor is it strictly a posteriori. That is why it is sometimes called *a simultaneo*. It proceeds from the examination of a concept: it makes explicit and puts into words what is implicitly contained in something which is known. Thus: John is Mary's brother; therefore he has the same father and mother as she. This is a triangle; therefore its three angles add up to two right angles. Some famous philosophers have used such a kind of reasoning in their attempt to establish the existence of God. When used for this purpose it is known as the "ontological argument." We shall discuss it thoroughly in a later part of the book.* Here I shall simply remark that the value of this kind of reasoning will depend on whether the concept which serves as its starting point is based on an undeniable experience or is merely a product of our mind. In the former case the reasoning may be valid; in the latter it is not.

*See pp. 64ff.

1. A Posteriori Demonstration of God's Existence

AMONG THE MANY a posteriori demonstrations of God's existence the most famous are the *quinque viae* (the five ways) of Thomas Aquinas. They have been endlessly presented, examined, refuted, defended, developed; they have given rise to an enormous literature, which I do not have to summarize or to evaluate.[1]

I shall present the First Way of St. Thomas as an example of an a posteriori proof and point out its strong points and its weaknesses.

> The first and most manifest way is the argument from motion. It is certain and obvious to the senses that some things are moved in the world. Now, whatever is moved is moved by another, since nothing is moved except insofar as it is in potency to that toward which it is moved, and since something moves insofar as it is in act. For to move is nothing but to make something pass from potency to act, which can be done only by a being that is in act. Thus that which is actually hot, as fire, renders wood, that is potentially hot, actually hot, and thus moves it and changes it. Now, it is not possible for the same thing to be simultaneously in act and in potency in the same respect, but only in different respects. Thus that which is actually hot cannot be at the same time potentially hot, but is at the same time potentially cold. Therefore it is impossible that something should move and be moved in the same respect and in

the same way, i.e. that it should move itself. Hence whatever is moved must be moved by another. If that by which it is moved be itself moved, it too must be moved by another. But we cannot in this way go on indefinitely, else there would be no first mover, hence nothing else that would move, since the subsequent movers move only because they are moved by the first mover. Thus the stick moves only because it is moved by the hand. Therefore, we must arrive at a first mover that is moved by no other. And everyone understands this to be God.[2]

A. Discussion of the First Way of Aquinas

Although the expression "Whatever is moved is moved by another" sounds old-fashioned and needs some explanation before being correctly understood by the modern reader, I shall keep it, because other more familiar expressions are either misleading or too cumbersome in a polysyllogism. However, I shall put it in a slightly different way. In English *to move* may be used transitively (to cause the motion of) or intransitively (to be in motion). In the following polysyllogism which summarizes the argument of St. Thomas it is used in both ways.

Whatever moves is moved by another (1).
But some things move (2).
Therefore they are moved by another.
But that other either moves or does not move.
If it does not move, it is an unmoved mover.
If it moves, it is moved by another.
But it is impossible to go on indefinitely from one moved
    mover to another moved mover (3).
Therefore we must finally arrive at an unmoved mover.
The unmoved mover is God (4).

The four numbered statements are the ones which must be examined and discussed. All the others follow logically or are evident. If we can firmly establish these four statements, the proof of St. Thomas is valid.

1. *Whatever moves is moved by another*. In everyday language "to move" in the intransitive sense means to pass from one part of space to another. In the philosophy of St. Thomas its meaning is much richer. A thing moves when it acquires a new determination, a new perfection, which it did not possess previously, or, in technical language, when it passes from possibility to actuality, from potency to act. In this sense its meaning is much wider than the modern one. It includes the motion of a car, the heating of a room, the changes in the stock market, the healing of a wound, the ripening of a fruit, the growing of a child, the development of a civilization, the acquisition of knowledge, the progress in virtue. The basic meaning of the expression is the following: whenever some reality acquires a new determination, a new perfection, a new quality which it did not possess before, it must have received it from some other reality that possessed this perfection.

It is therefore wider than the following more modern expressions: Whatever is caused, is caused by another, or, Whatever is made, is made by another. They have the further inconvenience of sounding like tautologies. "Whatever moves" might also be translated by "whatever changes," but the difficulty is then how to finish the statement. Shall we say "Whatever changes does so only under the active influence of something else"? This is correct, but rather clumsy, especially if we intend to use it in a polysyllogism. That is why I shall keep the formula of Aquinas and ask the reader to remember what it means.

The statement seems very easy to demonstrate. If a being acquires some new perfection which it did not possess before, it is obvious that it must have received it from some other being that possessed it. Otherwise the changing being would have to give itself a perfection that it did not possess. *Nemo dat quod non habet*: nobody can give what he does not have. In other words, Whatever moves is moved either by itself or by another. But it is not moved by itself, for, in this hypothesis, it would have at the same time to possess and not to possess the same determination. Therefore it is moved by another.

However, there is a serious flaw in this demonstration. The major—that is, Whatever moves is moved either by itself or by another—is not a perfect disjunction and therefore not evident at once. A perfect disjunction would be "is moved either by itself or not by itself." As the major now stands, there is another possibility which is overlooked: "Whatever moves is moved either by itself, or by another, or **by nothing.**" If you exclude "by nothing," you have admitted its contradictory: "whatever moves is moved by something." In other words, in order to demonstrate the statement, it must be shown that movement requires an explanation, that it is not self-explaining. It must be shown that the less perfect does not, by itself alone, produce the more perfect. St. Thomas took this for granted, and so does common sense. But many modern philosophers no longer admit this evidence, and science too seems to be willing to give it up, for instance, when it speaks of "emergent evolution." Even common sense at times does not seem so sure of it. Take this case. Humankind has made unbelievable progress in scientific knowledge over the centuries. There has been here a real passage from potency to act. From whom or what did mankind receive this new determination? Are we not inclined to say that it received it from itself?

This objection was already known to the ancient philosophers, although under a simpler form. They pointed to the phenomenon of life. They defined "life" as the ability which a being possesses of moving itself. But if a living being can move itself, it is no longer true that whatever moves is moved by another. The answer to the objection pointed out that a living being is never the *total* cause of its own movement. It differs from lifeless beings because it does not receive the totality of its movement from outside causes: it is not purely passive. It is a partial cause and explanation of its activities, but never its total cause. It needs food, oxygen, liquids, and so on. And it received its own being from another being. The statement may therefore be modified in this sense: Whatever moves is moved at least in part by another.

2. *Some things move.* St. Thomas called this immediately evident, and he referred to sense evidence. Here again the history of philosophy forces us to be more critical. We cannot use the most evident example, local movement, as a proof for the statement, since it may be due to inertia. Moreover, although displacement may be a new determination, it is hardly a new perfection. But there are many other instances where new perfections seem to accrue to beings: building a house, writing a book, the growth of a plant, of an animal or of a child, progress in knowledge.

As a matter of fact, it is contradictory to deny this statement. It is part of the basic certitudes of metaphysics, which one can deny only through an act which affirms it implicitly. He who denies this statement obviously passes from a stage where he was not thinking of it or denying it to a stage where he is doing both. He has acquired a new determination, a new perfection. He has moved. Therefore the movement of our mind in thinking is the undeniable instance of "some things move."

3. *It is impossible to go on indefinitely from one moved mover to another moved mover.* Our argument will lead up to God only if it can be shown that an endless series of subordinated causes is impossible or that at least it explains nothing. We notice that some things move on this earth, and we wish to explain that movement. We attribute it to a cause, which is supposed to explain the movement. But if this cause itself moves, it too requires an explanation. Can we not go on indefinitely in this way? No, for in that event we have no

explanation, we are not satisfied, the movement is never fully explained.

Here, however, we must introduce an important distinction between *essentially* subordinated causes and *accidentally* subordinated causes, between causes of *being* and causes of *beginning*. Two causes are essentially subordinated when the lower can operate only under the present influx of the higher. Thus the stone is moved by the stick which is moved by the hand; all the cars in a train can pull the following cars only because each one of them is actually being pulled by the preceding cars and by the engine. Two causes are accidentally subordinated when the lower cause depends on the higher one in some way, but not in the present exercise of its causality. Thus the person who moves the stick depends on his parents for existence, but not in the very act of moving the stick. And the stick depends on the tree it came from, but not in the act of moving the stone.

The importance of this distinction becomes evident from a simple consideration. The desk on which I am writing this was made by a carpenter. Suppose we admit that the world in which we live has been made by God. From the fact that the desk exists I am not allowed to conclude that the carpenter is still alive. Why then may I conclude to the existence of God from the existence of this world?

This shows the weakness of the reason which many people, more or less consciously, employ to justify their acceptance of the existence of God. It looks very much like the famous hen-and-egg argument. Every egg presupposes a hen, that presupposes an egg, that presupposes a hen, and so on. There must have been a first egg or a first hen, which was caused by no preceding hen or egg. Few people, it is true, would rely on such a simple demonstration. But quite a number derive their certitude of the existence of God from the existence of the world. This existence must be explained. The world does not explain itself; it must have been made by some omnipotent

being, and this being is God. There is some truth in this
argument if it is correctly understood. As a rule it is misunderstood: it is simply an extension of the egg-and-hen argument
on a cosmic scale. Instead of considering only one causal series
(that of our domestic fowl), it includes all the causal series
whose totality constitutes the universe. The present stage of the
universe is explained by the immediately preceding stage,
which is explained in its turn by the stage which preceded it, and
so on. There must have been a first stage, not preceded by a
previous one. And this first stage must have been the work of a
creator, of God.

This kind of reasoning is affected by the same weaknesses
as the hen-and-egg argument. It does not seem possible to
demonstrate that such a series could not go on indefinitely.
Even if this could be shown, the series does not require the
present existence of its initiator. Finally, since the universe is
not perfect, since none of its stages, including the first one, is
infinitely perfect, why would its cause have to be an infinitely
perfect cause?

We conclude that if we speak only of accidentally subordinated causes, of causes of beginning, we cannot show that it is
impossible to go on indefinitely from one moved mover to
another moved mover. Does the same apply to essentially
subordinated causes, to causes of being?

I do not think that it does. Causes of beginning may
produce their effect even when their own cause no longer
influences them, no longer exists. On the other hand, causes of
being must continually be influenced by their own cause of
being if they are to exist and to operate. Such causes act only
inasmuch as they are acted upon at the present moment by some
first cause. Should there be no first cause, there would be no
subordinate causes and no activity anywhere along the line. In
other words, in such a series the lower causes are only
transmitting agencies; the *producing* agency is the first cause.
Should there be no first cause, the transmitting agencies would

have nothing to transmit, since no activity would be produced. If an example of sorts is needed, a railroad train may do.

But could not the series of subordinated causes constitute a closed circle, in which every link transmits the action to the next one, without any first link? In this hypothesis the exercise of the causality must still be explained. Where does it originate? If in one of the links, that one would be the unmoved mover. If in the circle as a whole, then it would be the unmoved mover. If the causal influx comes from outside the circle, we would have to look outside of it for the origin of the motion.

We might put this in another way. There is a double direction of causality at work in our cosmos, a horizontal and a vertical one. The horizontal direction leads back into the past, with accidentally subordinated causes. Science does not even speak of causes, but simply of antecedents and consequents. Z follows upon Y, which follows upon X, and so on, indefinitely. This direction explains happenings, events, the origin (*fieri*) of things. It is used in the natural sciences. But there is also a vertical direction of causality, which does not lead back into the past, but which operates entirely in the present; it is metaphysical causality, with essentially subordinated causes, with causes of being (*causa essendi*), of being in existence. The *events* explained by the horizontal series happen to things, to *natures*. These things or natures are not self-explaining; they must be explained in their turn. Should someone claim that the things are explained by the horizontal series of causes, he makes them not only causes of beginning but also causes of being. In that case they explain not only the origin but even the present existence of every nature. In that case an indefinite regression would explain nothing. Every link in the horizontal series of causes is suspended vertically to causes or to a cause which explain(s) not simply the succession of the links but their very existence.

Quite a number of philosophers, while admitting that things have a cause of beginning, deny that they need a cause in being (*in esse*). Thus Professor Paul Edwards writes: "it is far from plausible on the other hand to claim that all natural objects require a cause *in esse*. . . . Most people would grant that particles like atoms did not cause themselves, since they would in that event have had to exist before they began existing. It is not at all evident, however, that these particles cannot be uncaused."[3] The author admits that *beginnings* must be explained, but he claims that being does not need any explanation. He is right when he states that many people share this opinion. They see that whatever comes to exist must have a cause, but they simply cannot see that even if a thing has always existed, it still must have a cause, or at least some explanation of its existence. They look for a cause of something that happens, but not of something that is. They are like people who admit that the start of daylight is explained by the rising of the sun. But if the light were shining without ever an interruption, they would be unwilling to admit that it is caused by the sun. They understand the need of explaining the beginning of daylight, while they feel no need of explaining its steady existence.

The reason for this state of affairs is the scientistic and positivistic mentality, the lack of metaphysical curiosity which affects so many minds, especially in the English-speaking world.[4] They hold that the only explanation which is required is a scientific explanation of things. But science explains how things originate, what they are made of, how their elements are combined and organized. It does not explain why things *are*, in the sense of What makes them be? here and now. Many people do not even understand what you mean when you ask such a question. It is one of the great difficulties of our task that the only way of reaching God by reason is in answer to a question which so many of our contemporaries do not even understand or reject as totally irrelevant.

So let us come back to the statement we are examining. "It is impossible to go on indefinitely from one moved mover to another moved mover." This statement cannot be demonstrated where causes of beginning or scientific antecedents and consequents are concerned. Science admits and must admit indefinite regression into the past or into the indefinite (in the analysis of matter). But where metaphysical causes, causes of being, are concerned, an indefinite regression is excluded.

How do we demonstrate this? It does not have to be demonstrated; it is immediately, intuitively evident. But some thinkers do not admit this. Thus Professor Paul Edwards speaks of a book Z that happens to be suspended 100 miles up in the air. It is supported by book Y, which is supported by book X and by 100,000 more books. Now, if after this library there is nothing more to support it, Edwards admits that the whole thing will come crashing down. But suppose that the series of books goes on indefinitely, why would Z not remain where it is? "A crash can be avoided either by a finite series with a first self-supporting member or by an infinite series."[5] It is obvious that my distinguished opponent rejects what I consider evident. Is he speaking of a series of causes that are essentially subordinated? Yes, to some extent, since every cause operates only while being itself acted upon by some other. But are these causes really causes of *being*? The series in question is one, not of things, of substances, but of states, of events (being suspended). Is Edward's hypothesis of an infinite series of *events* immediately, intuitively absurd? I am unwilling to affirm it. Would it not be so if the series were one not of events but of things, of substances? I think it is.

When an intuitive evidence is rejected in metaphysics, the only peremptory way of establishing this evidence is a *retortion*. However, retortions operate, not in the line of external, objective events, but only in the line of internal, subjective operations. And here our opponent might be vulnerable. When he rejects what I consider evident, I have a right to ask him for a reason for the rejection. I challenge the reason, and he comes up with another one. I challenge that one too, and the next one and the next one. Here also we have a series of essentially subordinated elements. They should lead up to a first, undeniable, self-supporting statement. If not, the objection is rationally not justified: it is a "dogmatic" objection, based not on evidence but on an option.[6]

This option is basically one for positivism. Whoever makes it rejects the fundamental difference between science and metaphysics. That is why it might be useful to say a few more words here about this difference. In the sciences there may be indefinite regressions. Accidentally subordinated causes, causes of beginning, antecedents and consequents may succeed each other indefinitely, either in the direction of the past (Z follows upon Y, which follows upon X, and so on, indefinitely) or in the direction of the indeterminate (molecules are made of atoms, that are made of protons and electrons, that are made of . . . and so on indefinitely). Science unravels more and more the innermost constitution of matter and the origins of life, but it will never finish the quest, because it is headed for the indefinite or the indeterminate.

Having granted that science's quest goes on indefinitely, I deny any such thing for the quest of philosophy, or, more precisely, for the quest of its innermost element, metaphysics. There is no longer any real quest here. The human intellect is aware of the limit as such, and this can be explained only through the fact that it is *now* poised toward infinity. In order to explain this I must revert to what has been said above about the relation between science and metaphysics. Philosophy is generally a hybrid, a mixture of metaphysics and science or of metaphysics and everyday knowledge. This makes the relation between philosophy and science difficult to explain.

The relation between metaphysics and science, on the other hand, although very intimate, is easier to explain. Since it is the same as that which obtains between everyday human knowledge and metaphysics (although there is, of course, a considerable and ever-widening difference between scientific and everyday knowledge), I shall speak of the difference between everyday and metaphysical knowledge, it being well understood that what I shall say applies also to the difference and the relation between scientific and metaphysical knowledge.

The relation then which exists between everyday and metaphysical knowledge is akin to that which exists between the undetermined and the determining, between the material and the formal cause, or—to put it perhaps more clearly, although with some danger of misunderstanding—between body and soul. According to the nondualistic interpretation of the relation between body and soul neither of them can exist alone: they need each other; they are strictly complementary. The body is a body only because and insofar as it is animated by the soul; likewise everyday knowledge is real intellectual and human knowledge (as distinguished from animal cognition) only because and insofar as it is animated by metaphysics. On the other hand, the soul, as we know it in this life (we know very little from philosophy about how it might exist in some other life), can exist only in union with the body, needs the body in some way for all its activities. In the same way metaphysics is impossible without everyday knowledge. Although the soul needs matter in all its activities, it reaches beyond it in some of them, in the activities of thinking and freely willing. Likewise, although metaphysical knowledge needs and feeds on everyday knowledge, it reaches beyond it.

Whenever the ordinary person goes about his or her daily work or whenever the scientist is engaged in research, the knowledge which continually guides them in their work is animated by metaphysical affirmations of which they are generally not aware. Thus when the nurse takes the temperature of a patient or the cytologist examines tissues, they implicitly affirm quite a number of things, among which I may mention the following: I exist, you exist, you are not I, I am myself, there are other people, there are things, I know people and things, I think, I affirm, I speak, I am certain of some things, I want certain things, some things are knowable, true, desirable, good. Notice that none of these implicit affirmations can be denied without contradiction (retortion). So this is not adventitious knowledge that comes to us from without; it is virtually inborn knowledge, of which we become aware more or less as soon as we become aware of things coming from without. Notice also that this knowledge accompanies and carries all our other knowledge and all our human activities. In that sense we may say that it is the soul of all our knowledge.

I insist upon this because one of the affirmations which we thus implicitly make in our intellectual contacts with reality is that of the finiteness of all the beings of our experience. The objects which we meet do not fill the capacity of our mind. And this is the case not only in the sense that we ask questions about them, about their origin, their nature, their purpose. This kind of question is generally addressed to the sciences, as it leads to the quest for antecedents or for components, and trails off into the indefinite or the undeterminate. But it also is the case in the sense that beings experienced are finite, that they are being*s*, not being.

Since our awareness of the limitation of everything we get to know is virtually inborn in us, so is the reason why we are aware of this finiteness, so is our transcending of all the finite toward the intensively Infinite. This shows that our knowledge of the Infinite is not something adventitious, coming to us from without, from a study of nature or from the testimony of others (although both of them may help us). It is virtually inborn in us; it is unthematically activated whenever we know anything.

The reader may have noticed that I have been unable to give a good example of a series of essentially subordinated causes, of causes of being. St. Thomas speaks of the hand that moves the stick that pushes the rock. Professor Edwards speaks of a pile of books suspended in the air. I have mentioned a railroad engine and the train it pulls, and also a series of statements that follow from each other. All these examples refer to causes of *states*, of *events*, of *activities*, not to causes of things, of substances. Why not give a series of causes of real beings, of substances? It is because such a series does not exist, at least if we are speaking of efficient causes. In the line of material causality it is perhaps possible to think of such a series. Thus a stick exists only as long as the cells that constitute the wood continue to exist, and these cells depend continually on the chemicals which constitute them.

We shall see later that God is the only efficient cause of all being. That is why, in my opinion, the mention of a series of (even essentially) subordinated causes in the proof of God's existence is misleading. Yet such a mention seems unavoidable, at least in the cosmological proofs, and St. Thomas makes it explicitly in the three first *viae*.

By way of conclusion to this lengthy discussion the following points seem to have been established. On the horizontal, phenomenal level of causes of beginning, in the scientific domain of antecedents and consequents, an indefinite regression into the past or the undetermined cannot be excluded. However, in the vertical direction, on the noumenal level of causes of being, St. Thomas was quite right when he wrote, "But this cannot go on to infinity, and therefore it is necessary to arrive at a first mover, moved by no other." And he adds, rather quickly in our opinion, "and this everyone understands to be God."

4. *The Unmoved Mover is God.* We know what is meant by this technical statement. The being that gives to all other beings their reality and their perfections, without receiving anything from any outside source, is the infinitely perfect necessary being. In other words, a being which "moves" all other beings, which makes them pass from potency to act, without being moved itself, without passing itself from potency to act, is Pure Act, infinite perfection.

But this statement, which may have been immediately

obvious to St. Thomas, within the context of his own total philosophy, is no longer obvious for us. We do not see at once how it follows, in the sense indicated above, from the demonstration that has been used. It is quite evident that a being which gives another being some perfection must in some way possess this perfection. But does this imply that such a being possesses absolutely all perfection, that it is an infinitely perfect being, without any limitation? Suppose that the whole universe possesses an amount of perfection designated by X. It is evident that the being which gave the universe this perfection should at least possess an equal amount of it. We might even easily grant that it should possess much more perfection, say X^{10}. But why should it be endowed with an infinite perfection?

Thus our demonstration has led us to an unmoved mover, a first cause, that possesses an immense amount of perfection, from which all perfections of the universe are ultimately derived and which has not received its own perfection from any other source.

Of this being St. Thomas says that "everybody understands (it) to be God." In his own thirteenth century this may well have been true. But it is no longer true today, and some more probing is required. We have arrived at a moved mover. We must admit that it is moved by another. But if this other is once more a moved mover, we face the same problem again. So either we must admit an indefinite regression (which has been excluded for essentially subordinated causes) or we must say that the final explanation can only be found in an unmoved mover, that is, in a being, says St. Thomas, who is Pure Act, Infinite Perfection. It is not too difficult to admit the first conclusion, that the explanation must lie in an unmoved mover. But why is this unmoved mover Pure Act, Infinite Perfection? This follows immediately for those who admit scholastic philosophy. An unmoved mover is a being devoid of all potency, hence a being who is Pure Act, infinitely perfect. But for those who are not familiar with or reject scholastic metaphysics, things are not so simple. They have a serious difficulty, which had already been brought up in the Middle Ages, by Ockham among others, and which Hume mentioned again: Does a moved mover, that is a finite being, require as its *efficient* cause an infinite being? The answer is obviously No. A finite effect does not require an infinite cause. We shall see, as we proceed, that the passage from unmoved mover to Infinite Being is legitimate, but it relies not on the principle of causality, as usually understood, but on another, more comprehensive and basic principle, the principle of intelligibility.

This principle does not simply state that whatever is moved is moved by another; it states that whatever is not intelligible by itself is intelligible only by being referred to that which is intelligible by itself. Or it can be put more simply: that which is not self-explaining must be explained by the Self-Explaining. Let us see how this principle operates in the present case. When we arrive, as an explanation of the universe, at a moved mover, our mind is not satisfied. Even if, impelled by this unsatisfaction, we admit the existence of an unmoved mover, but one who is finite and limited, our mind does not stop. Unless the unmoved mover is infinite, our mind is already beyond it. It is aware of the limitation of this being that is supposed to explain everything. It is aware of a limit. But in order to be aware of a limit as such, the mind must already be beyond it either in fact or at least in desire, in striving. Our mind strives past the finite unmoved mover, past anything finite, and in this way refers whatever it knows as finite to the ultimate aim of its striving, of its dynamism, to the infinite, the illimited.

Thus we see in what sense those who, as St. Thomas says at the conclusion of his First Way, understand the unmoved mover to be God are right. They have reached the existence of the unmoved mover by using the principle of efficient causality. But to pass from it to the Infinite Being, to God, they use, without being aware of it, the principle of intelligibility.

This transition from the principle of causality to the

principle of intelligibility is well explained by Maréchal in the following text:

> Several authors among the nominalistic Scholastics and among the moderns have mentioned, with respect to the demonstration of God as first cause, a difficulty which is not quite without weight.
>
> Thus the author of the *Theoremata* (a treatise long attributed to Duns Scotus) says: Let us admit that there are causes, and that, when they are essentially subordinated, we must stop at a first cause. What will be the perfection required in this first cause as cause? At least the intensive sum of the perfections of its effects, and nothing more. But the sum of the perfections of finite effects is finite. Therefore the infinity of perfection of the first cause cannot be demonstrated by the way of causality. Ockham too, through a slightly different reasoning, reaches a similar conclusion. Finally Kant, in his critical examination of the cosmological argument, speaks in a like vein. In order to show that this argument fallaciously leans on the ontological proof, he divides it into two theses: a) the conditioned object given in experience supposes an unconditioned condition, an uncaused cause, i.e. it demands a necessary being; b) the necessary being is identically the absolutely perfect being (God). Kant says that the second step can be made only by means of the argument known as "a priori." We do not wish to discuss whether this assertion is true. At any rate Kant's idea on this point leaves no doubt: at best the argument of causality leads up only to a first condition, which is necessary in the domain of existence; but necessary existence is not yet the existence of a unique and infinitely perfect Being. How is it possible, for instance, to demonstrate *analytically* that several necessary beings may not coexist? and so on.
>
> These criticisms seem instructive to us, because they show what a deformation a too external, too purely dialectical use of the principle of causality brings about. This deformation is quite understandable with philosophers affected by nominalism. If one is satisfied with the descriptive notion of *causality* as previous "conditioning" or with the notion of *necessity* as any

kind of impossibility of not being, it is very difficult, despite a vague feeling of evidence, to see why an uncaused cause, as first link of a chain of subordinated causalities, must be intensively infinite, or why existence should necessarily belong to a unique and absolutely perfect being.

St. Thomas and most Scholastics tell us why. It is important to notice the way they do it. The uncaused cause and the necessity of being designate, analytically, the strictly transcendent God, the unique Absolute, because in the metaphysics of Aquinas both terms (cause, necessity) express immediately the internal and fundamental relations of *being* in the line of act and potency. The uncaused cause is transcendent because it is pure actuality, the necessary being is infinite because it is being through its essence (*ens cujus essentia est esse*).

Is it the principle of causality which enables St. Thomas to make these identifications? Undoubtedly, but it is the principle of causality in its deepest sense, where it is an application of the first principle of being, "being is," i.e. being as being is by and of itself (*est de plein droit*). It is justified by its very position; it is totally intelligible. To affirm of anything whatsoever "it is," without affirming at least implicitly its perfect intelligibility, whether mediate or immediate, as *being,* would mean to formulate a false and contradictory judgment. Let us not confuse the metaphysical principle of transcendent causality either with the empirical principle of causality (this is obvious) or even with a certain symbolic transposition of our own voluntary activity. The analogy of our action may undoubtedly help us represent for ourselves how the causes operate internally, but does not provide us with any means of strictly demonstrating them through their effects. In order to demonstrate a transcendent cause by starting from a finite effect, our spirit must in this effect itself experience an objective limit. Not any kind of limitation, but a limitation of act or of *esse*. Only then will it dawn on it that the finite object is intelligible only by appealing to an infinite complement of intelligibility. The transcendent principle of causality expresses this complementary and simultaneous revelation of the objective contingency and of the Absolute that is its foundation, of the degree of being and of the eminent Perfection which measures it.

In order that this revelation may be possible in us two opposed conditions must operate: an empirical condition, the immanence in us of a finite object—and a transcendental condition, the latent, "natural" exigency of an intelligible absolute, of an "infinite." The meeting of these two elements reveals to reflective consciousness the intelligible inconsistency of the finite object, i.e. its contingency in being . . . . Something, deep down in our particular apperception, must determine and necessitate the affirmation of the transcendent Absolute, otherwise we would never, by starting from the finite objects, demonstrate the existence of the Infinite.[7]

This text shows that St. Thomas' First Way, as we have explained it, succeeds in establishing the existence of God, by using the principle of causality to arrive at an unmoved mover, at an unmade maker of the universe, and the principle of intelligibility to pass from this unmade maker to the Infinite, Perfect, Necessary Being, God.[8]

B. Vindication of the First Way of Aquinas

The question of its value depends therefore on the value of the two principles mentioned: the principle of causality and the principle of intelligibility. I have mentioned above how some philosophers tried to establish the former one. They argued as follows: Whatever moves is moved either by itself or by another. But not by itself. Therefore by another. And I have also remarked that this way of arguing holds only if we have a right to presuppose that "whatever moves, is moved by something."

Now this assertion is but an application of a wider one, which is known as the principle of sufficient reason or as the principle of intelligibility. Who will deny the statement Whatever moves is moved by something? Only he who claims that movement—that is, passing from potency to act, acquiring a new perfection—needs no explanation, just happens without there being a sufficient reason for it. To affirm, on the other hand, that every being, every reality, has to be explainable, has to have a sufficient reason for its occurrence, implies that "movement" too happens on account of something.

It follows that the above "demonstration" of the principle of causality is valid only if the principle of sufficient reason or the principle of intelligibility can be shown to be true. In the next chapter I shall try to show that the principle of intelligibility is one of the virtually inborn basic certitudes of life, part of the "soul" of our knowledge, that we "live" or "exercise" it in every affirmation and free action, so that denying it involves an implicit contradiction: it is an expression of the dynamism of our intellect.

Right now, however, I wish to present a simple vindication of the principle of intelligibility, as suggested by Professor Franz Grégoire. It agrees basically with the one I shall explain in the following chapter. Professor Grégoire claims that the principle is implicitly admitted as valid by everyone who considers that the question Why *is* this and why is it *that which* it is? is a universally legitimate question, one which we have a right to ask in the presence of every reality.

> In the presence of every being and of every state of being, in the presence of every element and every aspect of reality, the mind cannot help wondering: why does this exist rather than not exist and why is it this rather than that? For what motive, on account of what, in virtue of what is this and is it what it is? To accept this question as legitimate, as *universally* legitimate, is to accept the axiom which we call here the universal principle of the foundation of being,[9] which may be formulated thus: *whatever is, envisaged in its nature as well as in its existence, is on account of some being.* In other words, every positive element or aspect of reality possesses in some being the sufficient condition of its existence and of its whatness and, *in this sense,* everything has an explanation. In this sense too there

exists no "brute" being . . . . Another more explicit way of
formulating the axiom is this: Whatever is is either on account of
itself or on account of another . . . . A being is on account of
itself when it is the adequate sufficient reason of its existence.[10]

This principle, says the author, is self-evident if in the
presence of any reality whatsoever one is willing to inquire Why
is this being and why is it what it is? This may not be so evident
to everyone. We are looking for an explanation; we do not
discover any. Might we not conclude that there is no explanation? This conclusion does not follow from the fact that we do
not discover the explanation we are looking for. We might
decide to leave it at that; we might *decide* that there is no
explanation. This is not a logical conclusion made by the
intellect, but a voluntary choice made by the will. The intellect
continues to wonder, and the question is still there, but one
decides to repress it. We would hardly do this with unusual
events in everyday life. Suppose that you bump into a cow when
entering your living room. The question irresistibly comes up:
How did this creature ever get in here? Even if you should be
unable to find the answer, you will hardly conclude that there is
no explanation. You cannot help holding that there is an
explanation. What is true of unfamiliar things and events is true
also of the familiar ones, although in their presence we are not
so clearly aware of it.[11]

Let us, with Professor Grégoire, put it in another way.
Everybody must admit that each being is either caused or
uncaused, since this is a perfect disjunction. "Uncaused" is a
negative notion. Those who accept the above axiom pass then
from the negative notion "uncaused" to the positive notion
"self-existing" or "self-explaining." Those who reject the
axiom refuse to make this transition. In the presence of an
uncaused being they refuse to inquire Why does it exist?, for if
they accepted to inquire they would have to admit that there is a
reason for this being's existence, and the only possible answer
to their question would be: it is self-existing.

From the above considerations we may draw some interesting conclusions, which will prepare us to understand more easily the next chapter:

1. The validation of the principle of intelligibility is based on the forever inquiring nature of the human mind, on what we shall come to know as the dynamism of the intellect. Whenever it faces anything which is not self-explaining, our intellect looks for an explanation. If that which explains is not self-explaining, it will continue to look for an explanation. Its ultimate thrust is for the self-explaining. In this way each one of us "lives" or "exercises" the principle of intelligibility before putting it into words.

2. To consider the quest for explanations universally legitimate and to deny the principle of intelligibility implies a contradiction.

3. One may consciously and freely *decide* that, in the presence of certain realities, which do not explain themselves, one should no longer look for an explanation.

4. In such a case the intellect unconsciously, spontaneously and necessarily continues to ask for an explanation. The desire for an explanation is either (consciously) inhibited or (unconsciously) repressed. Such an inhibition or repression is the direct or indirect result of an option.

By way of conclusion I submit that the First Way of St. Thomas Aquinas may continue to lead the human mind all the way up to the necessary and infinitely perfect being whom we call God. It is useful, however, to make more explicit certain points which St. Thomas admitted implicitly and to establish certain points which he took for granted. Once this has been done, the proof holds.

St. Thomas' First Way, as usually presented, reaches God as the *Unmoved Mover* or the *First Cause*. Few people are inclined to worship an Unmoved Mover or a First Cause. The question naturally arises whether this being is really the God of religion.

However, as we tried to defend the proof of St. Thomas against some modern objections, we came to the conclusion that, in reality, we reach God, not as the Unmoved Mover or the First Cause, but as the Principle of all Intelligibility, a Principle which we do not actually grasp with our finite intellects, but one which we keep forever intending as lying beyond all that which we can grasp. In other words, we reach God as the Infinite Mystery. Now an Infinite Mystery may fill us more easily with the awe and the fascination that, according to Rudolf Otto, are the characteristic effects of the Holy on the human mind.

Therefore it may be worth our while to develop in more detail our approach to God through the dynamism of the intellect, not only in order to point out the peculiar nature of our proof but also in order to show that the Infinite Being whose existence we thus establish with our intellect is identically the Sacred Mystery that we may eventually come to worship with our heart.

2. Vindication of God's Existence through the Intellectual Dynamism

THE VINDICATION of the existence of God through the dynamism of the intellect is very simple and will be presented very briefly. This approach will then be considerably clarified and bolstered by the answer suggested to some of the many possible objections.

A. The Vindication

I affirm that God exists, that there is an infinitely perfect, necessarily existing being. If anybody challenges my right of doing this, I shall try to make a case for it in reason, without using faith or revelation, by pointing out to my opponent that not only I but he too cannot not affirm the reality of this being. Here is the way in which I shall try to do this.

Whatever reality we know in everyday experience we know as finite. I am finite, you are finite, our life is finite, this tree, this house, this city, this enterprise, this masterpiece, this country, this earth, all of them are finite. Now I can know them as finite, as limited, only because something in me is always already beyond them and strives beyond all limits, toward the unlimited.

We can know a limit as limit only by being, in some way, beyond it. The idea of "limit as limit" contains two elements: "until here" and "not further." The second element implies that something in me is already further. A man living in an immense, fenced-in domain does not know that his movements and the ground on which he lives are restricted and limited until he runs into the fence and wants to go beyond it or looks at what is beyond it. If my mind knows every reality with which it enters into contact, or might enter into contact, as limited, the only explanation of this undeniable fact can be that it strives beyond these limits, that the knowledge afforded by this reality does not satisfy it, that it wants more reality to know. And if this more happens to be limited in its turn, I am already beyond it with my intellect. It is not just this or that or the next limit which I thus transcend; it is every conceivable limit, it is the limit as such. The awareness of the finiteness of all that which enters my mind can be explained only by the fact that my intellect keeps pointing toward the illimited, the intensively infinite. That is the way, and the only way, in which I know God.

It is very important to keep in mind that this limitation is not a spatial or quantitative limitation. It may be a limitation of knowledge, of beauty, of love, of happiness. The awareness of spatial limitation cannot, by itself alone, lead us to God. Such a limitation is perceived by the senses, not directly by the intellect as such. The limitation which I have in mind is one concerning the fullness of being, of reality, of perfection. Spatial or quantitative limitation is only a sign of it.

The fact that I am aware of the limitation in being of whatever exists or may be conceived to exist this side of the infinite cannot be explained except by saying that my intellect—or, more precisely, I, through my intellect[1]—is naturally, congenitally, unavoidably poised toward the illimited, the infinite; that I keep forever striving for it, intending it, affirming it. By knowing all the finite as finite, I always co-know the Infinite.

But if I am a being who, by his innermost self, continually strives for the infinite, the infinite must at least be possible. It is inadmissible that a human being would be an embodied affirmation of the contradictory, of the impossible. Now we shall show that the infinite is noncontradictory, possible, only if it exists. Therefore a person's steady striving for the infinite implies that the infinite exists.

The human person might, in a strange definition consisting of three adverbs, be called the one who is "always already beyond." Beyond what? Beyond any conceivable truth, knowledge, beauty, goodness, happiness, perfection, being, beyond anything finite. This implies the existence of the infinite. The human person knows God in the way in which the Hudson River would, should it be aware of its own movement, know the Atlantic Ocean.

This is the very simple way in which I try to make a case in reason for God's existence through the dynamism of my intellect.

The argument might have been considerably extended and presented in a more lively and dramatic way. I might have pointed out how the human person is essentially restless, always looking for more pleasure, more wealth, more excitement, beauty, fulfillment, fame, power, success, knowledge, truth, love, happiness. The trouble with such a picture is that while it clearly shows that man is craving for more and ever more of all kinds of values, it does not show that he is striving for infinity. Might not the steady increase and progression satisfy him by itself? The quest seems to be indefinite, not aimed at infinity. It is precisely one of the most-often-recurring and most-difficult-to-answer objections against my position that both in the direction of the past (to explain a present state of affairs) and in the direction of the future (to explain the dynamism of the human mind) we may have to do with an indefinite regression or progression, not with a postulation or an anticipating grasp of the infinite. That is why I have presented the argument as soberly as possible, only in its essential lines.

I intend now to answer a few of the many objections which

come to one's mind when hearing this approach. Answering these difficulties may be the best way of expanding, clarifying and strengthening the argument.

B. Objections Against the Vindication

1. You claim that you arrive at God because of your awareness of the finiteness, the limitation of all the realities that you know. Yet if there exists for us another way of being aware that things are finite, a way which does not require any dynamism of the mind, your case collapses.

But there is such another way. We are aware that things are finite because there are many of them and they limit each other. Their obvious multiplicity is the only clue we need to know about their finiteness.

Several answers may be given to this objection.

a) It is true that one of the ways in which we may know that things are finite and limited is their diversity and multiplicity. The very fact that there are many of them implies that they are finite. But this applies only to material objects and to spatial limitation. It does not explain how we know that immaterial realities are finite too. We know of the finiteness of every knowledge, of every science, perfection, truth, beauty, love, happiness. This is no longer spatial limitation, but limitation in being. This finiteness is directly experienced by us when we become aware how strongly our thirst for more and ever more knowledge, science, truth, love, beauty and happiness exceeds everything that is given to us in experience.

b) Moreover, the objection does not apply to the universe as a whole. Of its very nature it is unique, since, by definition, it is constituted by the totality of that which we experience or might experience. The universe is finite, perhaps not in extension, spatially, but certainly in perfection, in being, ontically. The universe might be less imperfect: there might be less cruelty, hatred, suffering, unhappiness in it. The universe is finite, and we know this, not because it is limited by another universe, but only because our mind, when knowing it, is already beyond it. This may be what the early Wittgenstein had in mind when in his *Tractatus Logico-Philosophicus* he wrote cryptically: "To view the world *sub specie aeterni* is to view it as a—limited—whole. Feeling the world as a limited whole is the mystical."[2]

c) There is another way in which we may show that every reality which we know is implicitly known as limited. Of every such reality we affirm implicitly that it IS. But the predicate IS which we implicitly attribute to everything we know is too wide for it. We should not say: This tree IS, this man IS. Strictly speaking we should say: This tree is a tree, this man is a man. We must qualify, restrict their ISness. It does not come up to the width of the predicate IS. And so we are at once, at least implicitly, aware of their finiteness. The perception of several objects helps us become aware of what is already given implicitly in the perception of every single reality.

d) It is in a similar way that we may directly show that our intellect strives for the illimited without having to insist on the awareness of the limit as such. Our power of affirmation is as wide as that which is covered by the term 'IS'. Whatever IS may be known and affirmed by us. Now there is no limit to this object of our affirmation. Any limit would also BE and fall within its ambit. The only assignable limit would be nonbeing. To say that nonbeing is the only limit is to say that there is no limit to the range of our power of knowing and affirming. This power reaches to infinity.

2. I admit that we are aware of the finiteness of everything which we know and that this implies that there is in us a drive beyond any limitation. It does not follow that our mind is striving for the illimited. It merely implies that it is driven from one limited object to another one, that it is never satisfied with

anything it grasps. This is so, not because the mind is made for the infinite, but because it is made for endless striving. Its object is not the infinite, but the quest itself for its own sake. The human mind keeps striving for the indefinite, not for the infinite.

This is a serious objection, which deserves our attentive consideration. For centuries thinkers and artists have been aware of the restlessness of the human mind without concluding that it is made for infinity. The infinite for which the human mind is striving would not be the true infinite, but what Hegel calls the bad or spurious infinite, the indefinite, the infinite of the mathematicians.

The first and, to my mind, the most convincing reply to this objection points out that it is not this limit or that one or the next one, but it is *the limit as such,* any real or conceivable limit which is at once transcended by the intellect. The passage from finite to infinite is not gradual but immediate. It is not because this or that amount or intensity of knowledge, goodness, truth, beauty, happiness is not sufficient that our mind does not find rest; it is simply because it is finite. The dynamism of the human mind strives for all-out infinity.

Thoroughly discussing this problem, Professor F. Grégoire admits that we frequently discover in the human mind a craving for always more truth, knowledge, beauty, happiness and so on, for what he calls "the indefinitely higher realization of values."[3] But he claims that such an indefinite progression is possible only with a background of infinity. "Only *because* the spirit is *first* openness for, an implicitly, prereflectively conscious openness for the illimited Unknown, is the spontaneous indefinite progression (one which is conscious of being indefinite) possible and actually occurring."

He makes an important distinction in connection with man's dynamism between its *noema* and its *noesis,* between the progression as it unfolds in time and its present root in man. He admits that if we consider its noema, if we look at it as a "thought thought," we may not have to envisage the necessity, in such a progression, of a *determined* limit. Only a limit in general may be required, so that one is not forced to admit that it is heading for the infinite.

However, when we consider the progression in the human mind itself, in its noesis, as a "thinking thought," as an actual datum, we must admit that

> an actual datum is either *limited* in a *determined* way, or illimited. In the domain of the actual the idea of an undetermined limitation is unthinkable. Now the spirit itself, with its openness, its active intending, is an actual datum. It follows that if the spirit were not infinitely open, it could be open only in a *determined* finite way, its expectation would have such or such a concrete limit. By the same token the idea of an indefinite ascension in the values would be impossible for it. We must therefore consider the spirit as a dim yearning for the infinite, whose influence shows as the explicit yearning for the indefinite.[4]

In other words, in the yearning of our intellect (and the same applies to our will) we may distinguish the *yearned for* (noema) and the *yearning* (noesis). The *yearned for* is not actually given; it is that which we hope to reach in the future. It might be undetermined, indefinite. But the *yearning* is taking place now; it is an actual reality. And an actual reality has to be determined. Its range, its degree of openness, cannot be undetermined; it is either finite or infinite. Our awareness of every limit as limit shows that it is infinite.

3. Suppose that I admit that every time I get to know some reality, I affirm the existence of the Absolute. Suppose that this is to be explained through the fact that by means of my intellect I keep striving beyond any limited for the Illimited, for the Infinitely Perfect Being. This does not imply that such a being exists. Many people strive for things that do not exist, that will

never exist. Striving for some object does not imply that this object really exists.

This is true. What it implies, however—when the striving is not artificial, when, as in the present case, it is natural, congenital, given with human nature—is that the striving is not absurd, that its object is not contradictory, that the Infinitely Perfect is at least possible. A mentally deranged person may desire things that are contradictory, as, for instance, to be a talking horse or a square circle. But that every person would in all one's dealings as a human being be prompted by a desire for the contradictory is simply inadmissible. This would mean that we establish the absurd at the core of human thinking.

But are there not thinkers, especially among the existentialists, who do not shrink from doing precisely this, from putting absurdity at the center of human life? There are indeed such thinkers, but their position is unacceptable for several reasons.

a) They accept that where the very core and purpose of human life are not concerned, the human mind can think and reason without falling into absurdity. Otherwise they would not write papers and books and expect people to read and try to understand them. They would not engage in conversation and discussion. But to call the peripheral activities of the human mind sound and its central thrust absurd is hard to admit.

b) It is not possible to claim without contradiction that life as a whole is absurd, at least not in the sense that everything is absurd, for this assertion would be self-denying, since it itself would be included among the things called absurd. "Some things make sense" is a virtually inborn certitude of the human mind, which cannot be denied without contradiction. It seems difficult to deny that among them must be the natural striving of our intelligence.

However, does the fact that I undeniably admit that my intellect congenitally, of its very nature, affirms the possibility of the unlimited, perfect being imply that this being is real?

Reality implies possibility, but possibility does not imply reality.

This is always true, except in the case of the infinitely perfect being. If this being is positively, objectively possible—that is, if we do not simply not see why it would not be possible (negative, subjective possibility), but if we have a good solid reason for affirming its possibility—this being exists. This being is positively possible only if it exists. If this being does not exist, then it is not possible either, and its very idea is contradictory. This requires, of course, some explanation.

C. If God Is Possible, He Exists

Since this is an important step of the case I am trying to make in reason for my right of affirming the existence of God, I intend to examine it thoroughly.

It would, of course, be much simpler to pass directly from the dynamism of my intellect to the existence of God. This might be done in the following way. The striving of my mind for the illimited must be explained. It is due to something within or without me. It cannot be something within me: since my nature is finite, how could a craving for the infinite derive from it? Thus, that which causes this craving must be outside of me. There is a reality distinct from me which produces in me this illimited dynamism of my intellect. This reality cannot be finite, for how could a finite being put into me a craving for infinity? Therefore the infinitely perfect being exists. Only such a being can explain the existence in me of the craving for the infinite.

This proof looks somewhat like the one Descartes proposed in his *Discourse on Method*, Part IV.

> After that I reflected upon the fact that I doubted, and that, in consequence, my spirit was not wholly perfect, for I saw clearly that it was a greater perfection to know than to doubt. I decided to ascertain from what source I had learned to think of

something more perfect than myself, and it appeared evidently that it must have been from some nature which was really more perfect . . . . To derive it from nothingness was manifestly impossible, and it is no less repugnant to good sense to assume that what is more perfect comes from and depends on the less perfect than it is to assume that something comes from nothing, so that I could not assume that it came from myself. Thus the only hypothesis left was that this idea was put in my mind by a nature that was really more perfect than I was, which had all the perfections that I could imagine, and which was, in a word, God.[5]

It seems to me that we may even accept this "demonstration" more easily than the First Way of St. Thomas. For in the latter the effect to be explained is finite, and it is difficult to see why a finite effect demands for its explanation an infinite cause. In the present case, on the other hand, there is an aspect of infinity in the effect (an idea of infinity with Descartes, a striving for the infinite in my presentation). There is a compelling reason in the present case why the cause which is demanded should be infinite.

Why then not simply stop here and forego the detour over the mind's dynamism? The reason is that the weaknesses which modern philosophers point out in the traditional arguments can be remedied only by a consideration of our intellectual dynamism. This is done briefly in the way of arguing which I have suggested above. It remains useful, however, to do it more thoroughly. Such a more thorough presentation shows a great resemblance to the "ontological argument." That is why my next step is a consideration and discussion of this argument.

D. The Ontological Argument

This argument, which proceeds strictly neither a priori nor a posteriori, has for this reason sometimes been called a demonstration *a simultaneo*. It has a long and brilliant history.[6] The first one who used it was St. Anselm of Canterbury (1033–1109).

> Whatever is understood, exists in the understanding. And assuredly that than which nothing greater can be conceived cannot exist in the understanding alone. For, suppose it exists in the understanding alone; then it can be conceived to exist in reality, which is greater.
>
> Therefore, if that than which nothing greater can be conceived, exists in the understanding alone, the very being, than which nothing greater can be conceived, is one, than which a greater can be conceived. But obviously this is impossible. Hence, there is no doubt that there exists a being, than which nothing greater can be conceived, and it exists both in the understanding and in reality.[7]

Let me, to make the discussion easier, put this argument in the form of a syllogism:

> The greatest conceivable being exists in reality.
> But God is the greatest conceivable being.
> Therefore God exists in reality.

The minor is evident. Should somebody question the major, Anselm would argue as follows: If your "greatest conceivable being" does not exist in reality, then it is not the greatest conceivable being, since you can think of it and add real existence to it, and this would be the greatest conceivable being.

The difficulty with this clever bit of reasoning, and the reason why it has been so widely rejected, is that it starts with a concept and it can only lead up to a concept. It starts with the "concept of the greatest conceivable being," and it ends up with the "idea of such a being as existing in reality."

Hence, if we return to our syllogism, we shall answer as follows "in form," that is, according to the rules of scholastic disputations:

The greatest conceivable being exists in reality. I distinguish: The greatest conceivable being must be *thought of* as existing in reality. I grant this. The greatest conceivable being *really* exists in reality. I subdistinguish: This may be demonstrated by a mere examination of its concept. I deny this. And this might be demonstrated in some other way. I grant this.

But God is the greatest conceivable being. I grant this.

Therefore God exists in reality. I distinguish, as in the major. God must be thought of as existing in reality. I grant this. God exists really in reality. This has not been demonstrated.

In other words, the idea of God contains the idea of necessary existence. But it has not been shown that to the idea of God there corresponds some reality; it has not been shown that we must necessarily affirm this idea. This can be done only by starting from experience, from an undeniable fact of experience. Facts of experience are not known by means of mere concepts or ideas. We know them through judgments or affirmations backed up by intuition (either sense intuition or an intellectual intuition). I shall try to use Anselm's way, but I shall start, not from an idea, but from an undeniable fact of experience, known from intellectual intuition, the dynamism of the human intellect.

The ontological argument has also been used by Descartes (1596–1650) in connection with the idea of the supremely perfect being which he discovered in his mind.

> It is certain that I no less find the idea of God, that is to say, the idea of a supremely perfect Being, in me, than that of any figure or number whatever it is; and I do not know any less clearly and distinctly that an actual and eternal existence pertains to this nature than I know that all that which I am able to demonstrate of some figure or number truly pertains to the nature of this figure or number, and therefore, although all that I concluded in the preceding Meditations were found to be false, the existence of God would pass with me as at least as certain as I have ever held the truths of mathematics to be.[8]

And again,

> That which we clearly and distinctly understand to belong
> to the true and immutable nature of anything, its essence or
> form, can be truly affirmed of that thing; but, after we have with
> sufficient accuracy investigated the nature of God, we clearly
> and distinctly understand that to exist belongs to His true and
> immutable nature; therefore we can with truth affirm of God that
> he exists.[9]

To this argument of Descartes a group of seventeenth-
century philosophers and theologians objected by showing the
weakness of the ontological argument and also one way in
which this weakness might be obviated. It is precisely this way
which I intend to use.

Here is the objection of these Renaissance thinkers:

> This was how you propounded your argument. "We may truly
> affirm of anything, that which we clearly and distinctly perceive
> to belong to its true and immutable nature; but (after we have
> investigated with sufficient accuracy what God is) we clearly
> and distinctly understand that to exist belongs to the nature of
> God." The proper conclusion would have been: "therefore
> (after we have investigated with sufficient accuracy what God
> is) we can truly affirm that to exist belongs to God's nature."
> Whence it does not follow that God actually exists, but only that
> he ought to exist if His nature were anything possible or not
> contradictory. . . . All this may be reduced to that argument
> which is stated by others in the following terms: —If it is not a
> contradiction that God exists, it is certain that He exists; but His
> existence is not a contradiction; hence . . . . But a difficulty
> occurs in the minor premise, which states that God's existence is
> not a contradiction, since our critics either profess to doubt the
> truth of this or deny it. Moreover that little clause in your
> argument ("after we have sufficiently investigated the nature of
> God") assumes as true something that all do not believe; and
> you know that you yourself confess that you can apprehend the
> infinite only inadequately.[10]

In his reply Descartes claims:

> the nature of God, as I have described it, is possible, because I
> have assigned nothing to it that we did not clearly and distinctly
> perceive ought to belong to it, and consequently it cannot be in
> disagreement with our thought.[11]

The critics of Descartes are right. Since we cannot
adequately grasp the divine nature, we cannot tell, simply by
examining it in our mind, whether or not the idea of an Infinitely
Perfect Being is contradictory. We do not perceive any contradiction (it is negatively possible), but the idea is surrounded
by a haze, which might well hide contradictions. We cannot
arrive at the positive possibility of God by a mere examination
of his idea. But if we should be able to establish it in some other
way, based on experience, the argument would be valid.

Another outstanding philosopher who has used the ontological argument is Leibniz (1646–1716). He wrote about the
use Descartes had made of it:

> It is not a paralogism, but it is an imperfect demonstration,
> which assumes something that must still be proved in order to
> render it mathematically evident; that is, it is tacitly assumed
> that this idea of the all-great or all-perfect being is possible, and
> implies no contradiction. And it is already something that by
> this remark it is proved that, *assuming that God is possible, he
> exists,* which is the privilege of divinity alone. We have the right
> to presume the possibility of every being, and especially that of
> God, until some one proves the contrary. So that this metaphys-
> ical argument already gives a morally demonstrative conclu-
> sion, which declares that according to the present state of our
> knowledge we must judge that God exists.[12]

Elsewhere Leibniz tried to demonstrate that the idea of
God is not contradictory, that God is possible. He too,
however, tried to do this through a mere examination of
concepts, and the difficulties mentioned in connection with the
attempt of Descartes apply also to him. The case would be quite

different if the possibility of God were implied in an undeniable experience. This is precisely the way in which I am trying to establish that God is possible, that the concept of an infinitely perfect being is not contradictory. An examination of the movement of our intellect has shown us that our intellect implicitly affirms the possibility of God every time it affirms something. Thus the possibility of God is not arrived at by a mere examination of concepts but is implied as an undeniable fact of everybody's experience, the dynamism of the intellect.

At present the ontological argument is again attracting considerable attention and provoking much discussion. What follows is the way Professor James F. Ross has recently put it.

1. Every logically contingent state of affairs is heteroexplicable.
2. That there exists an uncausable and unpreventable being is not heteroexplicable.
3. Therefore, it is not a contingent state of affairs.
4. But it is a logically consistent state of affairs that there exists an unproducible and unpreventable being.
5. Whatever state of affairs is consistent but not contingent is logically necessary.
6. Hence it is a logically necessary state of affairs that there exists an uncausable and unpreventable being.
7. What is logically necessary is actually so; therefore, there exists an unproducible and unpreventable being.

This is an *a priori* argument based upon the exclusive disjunction of all states of affairs as necessary, impossible, or contingent. It is assumed that what is in question is not impossible and it is demonstrated that it is not contingent; from which it follows that it is necessary. Apart from the assumption that it is consistent to say that some thing which exists is unproducible and unpreventable, the two key assumptions of the argument are (1) that every contingent state of affairs is heteroexplicable and (2) that whether there exists an unproducible and unpreventable being is not heteroexplicable. We shall, therefore, consider each of these.[13]

The readers of the present work will easily accept these two assumptions as soon as they understand them. Assumption (1) is a new way of stating the principle of causality or of sufficient reason. "Heteroexplicable" means "explainable by something else." If we put assumption (2) in traditional language, it will read as follows: The necessary being cannot be explained by something else; it is self-explaining. Here is how the author summarizes the way he demonstrates this assumption: "The existence or non-existence of a thing is heteroexplicable only through states of affairs which cause or prevent it. It is, therefore, analytic that any state of affairs which is unproducible and unpreventable is not heteroexplicable."[14]

That this is indeed a new form of the ontological argument is easy to show. We are told that it is an a priori argument, not in the sense, of course, that it deduces the existence of God from something that is prior to God, but in the sense that it is not based on sense experience, but simply examines the concept of "uncausable and unpreventable being." Moreover, we are told that the argument assumes "that it is consistent to say that some thing which exists is unproducible and unpreventable," in other words, that the necessary being, that God, is possible.

It has been shown above why this assumption is unwarranted. Should it, however, be possible to show in some other way that the infinite and necessary being is possible, the argument presented by Professor Ross would be a valid demonstration of God's existence.

If God is possible, he exists. This does not mean that God's existence derives from his possibility. It means that God's positive possibility implies, as a previous condition, his existence. If God does not exist, he is not possible either. The only way in which God is possible is for him to exist.

Most philosophers admit this. Let me try as briefly and as simply as possible to explain why this is evident. We may distinguish two more kinds of possibility, which will be called *extrinsic* and *intrinsic* possibility. A being is *extrinsically* possible if it either exists or can be made to exist. Thus a square circle is extrinsically impossible. None exists, and nobody, not even God, can make one to exist. But a pond full of beer is extrinsically possible. Although none seems to exist, the combined breweries of Milwaukee might, if they set their mind to it, bring one about.

A being is *intrinsically* possible if its concept is not contradictory, if its constitutive notes do not exclude each other. Here again a square circle is impossible, as is a male sister, whereas a pond full of beer or a golden mountain are possible.

Now in both the meanings of the word 'possible' God is possible only if he exists. He is extrinsically possible if he either exists or somebody may cause him to exist. Since the latter is at once excluded, the only way for God of being extrinsically possible is to exist. God is also intrinsically possible only if he exists. We have agreed that the God for whose existence I am trying to make a case in reason is the infinitely perfect, necessarily existing being. Now a nonexisting necessarily existing being is contradictory. It follows that according to both meanings of the word 'possible' God is possible only if he exists, which is the same as to say: If God is possible, he exists.

E. The Objections of Kant

Against this whole line of reasoning the strongest objections come from no mean philosopher; they come from Immanuel Kant. He rightly rejected the ontological argument, because it unduly passes from the conceptual to the real order. But he also denied that the possibility of God implies his existence. Kant is not easy to understand and to explain. If I try to explain him simply and briefly—and that is what I am supposed to do in a work like this—the danger of oversimplifi-

cation and unfairness is very great. The reader who is afraid of
this danger is invited to study Kant's works in the original.
Since I cannot simply ignore Kant's objections to this important
element of my "vindication," I must run the risk of over-
simplifying him.

1. Kant denies that the nonexistence of an absolutely
necessary being is unthinkable. Or rather, he claims that we do
not have to affirm the existence of such a being.[15] If we thus
refrain from thinking of it, there can be no contradiction.

> If, in an identical proposition, I reject the predicate while
> retaining the subject, contradiction results; and I therefore say
> that the former belongs necessarily to the latter. But if we reject
> subject and predicate alike, there is no contradiction; for nothing
> is then left that can be contradicted. To posit a triangle and yet to
> reject its three angles, is self-contradictory; but there is no
> contradiction in rejecting the triangle together with its three
> angles. The same holds true of the concept of an absolutely
> necessary being. If its existence is rejected, we reject the thing
> itself with all its predicates; and no question of contradiction can
> then arise.[16]

We see that Kant admits here that the idea of a nonexisting
necessary being is contradictory. In other words, if we
hypothetically posit it, we run into a contradiction. He is right
when he claims that there is no contradiction if we do not affirm
it, if we reject it.

But my previous explanations have shown that we cannot
not *affirm* the existence of an infinite, illimited and therefore
absolutely necessary being. We implicitly coaffirm its existence every time we affirm the existence of a finite reality, and
hence also every time we perform a human action. Kant denied
this because he held a *static* conception of knowledge. It is
undeniable in a *dynamic* conception of knowledge.

2. Here is Kant's second objection:

> We have thus seen that if the predicate of a judgment is
> rejected together with the subject, no internal contradiction can

result, and this holds no matter what the predicate may be. The only way of evading this conclusion is to argue that there are subjects which cannot be removed, and must always remain. That, however, would only be another way of saying that there are absolutely necessary subjects; and that is the very assumption which I have called in question, and the possibility of which the above argument professes to establish. For I cannot form the least concept of a thing which, should it be rejected with all predicates, leaves behind a contradiction.[17]

To this I submit the following reply. There are a few realities which cannot be denied without at least an implicit contradiction. Thus to say "I do not exist" obviously implies a contradiction. Nor can we deny the non-I, the world. For we would perform a denial by means of concepts and words that do not completely come from the I. And when we are engaged in a discussion (and Kant obviously is), it is impossible to deny You, the other person. These are subjects "which cannot be removed, and must always remain," at least as long as the philosophical discussion is on. This last restriction shows, it is true, that these subjects are not the "absolutely necessary subjects" of which Kant speaks. They become absolutely necessary as soon as we speak or think. And this seems to be sufficient to take care of Kant's objection, since he writes, "For I cannot form the least concept of a thing which, should it be rejected with all its predicates, leaves behind a contradiction." It seems to me that I can form such concepts. They are very special concepts, to be sure, since they refer to individual realities, I, the world, you. But unless we are willing to admit that we have no knowledge whatsoever of these basic realities, it is difficult to see how we do not have of them concepts of sorts.

Kant would be right, nevertheless, if the only kind of contradiction which exists were a logical contradiction, a contradiction between concepts. To say "I do not exist," "You do not exist," "The world does not exist," "The Infinite Being does not exist" implies no such contradiction. But it implies an unthematic, lived, contradiction, one which occurs between the content of the affirmation and the act of affirming. When I say "I do not exist," the I whose existence is denied does the denying. When I say "You do not exist," the You whose existence is denied is being addressed. When I say "The Infinite Being does not exist," my intellect can perform this act of denying only because it intends the Infinite Being.

We may well wonder how it is possible that a profound thinker like Kant overlooked these things. It seems that his rationalistic background made him overlook the act of thinking for the content of it. He paid attention almost exclusively to the *content* of thought and ignored the performance of thinking. Despite his frequent use of a dynamic sounding terminology his conception of knowledge was too static.

3. I have insisted that "existence" or "being" is part of the concept of infinitely perfect reality. Kant objects that

> *Being* is obviously not a real predicate; that is, it is not a concept of something which could be added to the concept of a thing. It is merely the positing of a thing, or of certain determinations, as existing in themselves . . . . Otherwise stated, the real contains no more than the merely possible. A hundred real thalers do not contain the least coin more than a hundred possible thalers. For as the latter signify the concept, and the former the object and the positing of the object, should the former contain more than the latter, my concept would not, in that case, express the whole object, and would not therefore be an adequate concept of it.[18]

As usual, Kant is to a great extent right in what he affirms. It would, for instance, not make any sense to add to the definition of, say a dime, as a small, silver, United States coin, of the value of 10 cents, that it "exists" or is "a being." Nothing is added to the *concept* of a reality when existence or being is added to it. The same, however, is not true when we add the note of "*necessary* existence." To call a reality "existing" in no way distinguishes it from other existing realities, whereas calling it "necessarily existing" distinguishes it wholly from all of them.

Having thus examined Kant's main objections to the assertion, accepted by so many philosophers, that "if God is possible, he exists," we may conclude that the objections do not invalidate it. It remains true that to establish the positive possibility of the Infinite Being, as I have tried to do, is tantamount to establishing his existence.

Kant is the main adversary in every attempt to make a case in (theoretical) reason for the existence of God. That is why it may be worth our while to consider another difficulty which he has brought up.*

He claims that all the cosmological proofs of God's existence are invalid not only because of their unwarranted use of the principle of causality but also because they use the ontological argument. By means of the principle of causality they arrive at the existence of a necessary being. Then they try to show that this necessary being is the infinitely perfect being. But if the necessary being is the infinitely perfect being, the opposite is true too: the infinitely perfect being is the necessary being: it exists necessarily. And this, says Kant, is the ontological argument.

This may look like quibbling, especially when we keep in mind that the cosmological argument avoids precisely that which constitutes the real weakness of the ontological argument: passing from one concept to another and hoping in this way to reach reality. As its very name implies, the cosmological argument starts not with a concept, but from experience. Hence the necessary being at which it arrives is not a mere concept, but a reality demanded to explain an undeniable experience.

However, Maréchal[19] has pointed out that Kant seems to have had something else in mind, although he did not explain it too clearly. What he wanted to say seems to have been this: We tend naturally to consider "transcendental ideas" as clear ideas,

---

*Beginners in philosophy would be well advised to skip this section. It is not required for an understanding of what follows.

which stand for precisely determined realities. But Kant is convinced that, outside of the domain of sense experience, there is only one concept that is totally determined, to which might correspond a reality. This concept is the "Ideal of Reason."

This requires a few words of explanation. Kant has introduced into philosophy the transcendental method, which investigates the conditions of the possibility of our thinking. He discovered first the a priori forms of our senses, external and internal, space and time. Next were investigated the categories of the understanding, through which the diversity of sense experience, as informed by space and time, is connected with the third condition of possibility, the transcendental apperception, that is, the referring of all knowledge to the I as the knower. This referring introduces some subjective unity into our knowledge, since whatever is known is referred to the I as the knower. But there is also some objective unification which takes place: the many data of experience are subsumed under three unifying Ideas: the soul, the world and God. These are the "transcendental Ideas" mentioned above. And these Ideas themselves are in their turn unified by being subsumed under the "Ideal of Reason," the concept of *"ens realissimum"* (the most real being, the fullness of reality).

Back now to Kant's objection. He claims that there are two steps in the cosmological argument. First human reason tries to establish the existence of a necessary being, one whose existence is unconditioned. Next it endeavors to find "the concept of something which might be independent of every condition, and it finds the concept of something which contains the sufficient condition of every other thing, i.e. which is the principle of all reality . . . (*ens realissimum*, supreme being). Then reason concludes that the supreme being exists with absolute necessity, as the fundamental principle of all things."[20]

There are two steps therefore: (1) from experience to a necessary being and (2) from this necessary being to the infinite being, to God. Kant claims that reason fails in both attempts. It fails because of the following reasons, all of which go back to the same basic error: (a) using the category of causality outside of the domain of sense experience; (b) taking for granted that the transcendental idea of God is so completely determined that to it corresponds a well-defined reality; (c) considering this transcendental idea as constitutive of our thinking.

I shall briefly take up each of Kant's objections and then suggest a direction in which these objections might be met. I do not claim to refute them. One does not refute a profound thinker like Kant in a couple of lines!

a) *The objection:* using the category of causality outside of the domain of phenomena. Unlike Hume, who denied that a causal relationship can be known with certainty and who reduced it to a mere sequence of events of which we become aware through an association of ideas, Kant has shown that in the domain of phenomena, of sense experience, the principle of causality is an a priori condition of the possibility of our knowledge and, as such, absolutely undeniable. But he also claimed that outside of the domain of sense knowledge the principle loses its validity: its use is illegitimate.

Suggested response: I have tried to show above that the principle of causality is but a particular form of the principle of intelligibility. Since the latter is "exercised" in the dynamism of the intellect, it is, even as principle of metaphysical causality—that is, as applied outside of the domain of sense experience, to beings as they are in themselves—an a priori condition of the possibility of human thought and, as such, undeniable. Kant's mistake, here again, was to have overlooked the *dynamic* aspect of human knowledge.

b) *The objection:* taking for granted that the transcendental idea of God is so completely determined that it corresponds to a well-defined reality. For Kant the transcendental ideas, including the idea of God, do not designate a reality; they only point to an inaccessible limit of the series of data from experience. A is conditioned by B, which is conditioned by C, and so on. The series of conditioned conditions points toward an unconditioned condition of existence in general. We call this the unconditioned, the necessary being. The conditioned conditions are given to us in experience, but not the unconditioned condition. We are not allowed to take it for granted that this idea of the unconditioned condition, of the necessary being, is so completely determined that to it there corresponds one well-defined reality.

> Let us dissipate the "transcendental illusion" created in us by the image of a necessary being that may be defined through concepts. "Necessary being" or better "necessity of existing" is at first only a transcendental note of the real series of phenomena . . . the stamp of necessity put on existence in general, not, however, the representation of a privileged existence. It might become something which is objective only by fastening to an "object," *by being incorporated into a concept that is entirely defined,* for instance, into the concept of *ens realissimum.* Such an assimilation should be a priori and analytic.[21]

Suppose therefore that we had duly established that there is an "absolute necessity of existence." And suppose that we were allowed to equate this absolute necessity of existence with the *ens realissimum* (not a vague undetermined concept like the former one, but a well-defined idea), then we would have demonstrated the existence of God. We are strongly inclined to make this transition from the vague "necessary being" to the "fullness of reality," but it cannot be shown to be a logically valid transition.

Suggested response: I have mentioned a similar difficulty in connection with the First Way of St. Thomas, where the passage was made from an "unmoved mover" to "God." And I admitted that this transition was not valid if the principle of causality was used in its current, rather restricted meaning. Finite effects do not need an infinite cause. But, following the lead of Maréchal, I claimed that when the principle of causality is taken in its fullest meaning, where it coincides with the principle of intelligibility, the transition is valid.

c) The objection: considering the transcendental idea of God as constitutive of our thinking, whereas it is only regulative of it. Kant admits that we have a natural tendency to affirm the existence of God (the transcendental illusion). Moreover, this illusory affirmation has a function in our intellectual life. It proposes to our mind a problematic concept of the Infinite Being, as a reality that is conceivable and whose existence we would accept if valid reasons were given that force us to admit its existence. But he denied that any such reasons exist in the line of *theoretical thought*. In that sense he is agnostic. But there are valid reasons in the line of *practical* thought. Without an affirmation of the existence of God there can be no real morality. Now the existence of an absolute moral order is undeniable, and since God is a necessary postulate of this order, we have a right to affirm his existence. But what happens if somebody denies the existence of an absolute moral order or claims that such an order can be known only as a consequence of the existence of God?

Kant would admit that the affirmation of the existence of God is theoretically valid if, instead of having only a *regulative* function in our thinking, it possessed a *constitutive* function. In other words, he claims that we affirm God's existence only after we have affirmed the existence of the objects of our experience. The idea of God allows us to put some order in these ideas (regulative function). If it were possible to show that we can affirm these objects only *if and inasmuch as* we affirm the existence of God, then our affirmation of God would be valid and possess a theoretical value. It would then have a constitutive function in our knowledge and be an a priori condition of the possibility of any object in our mind.

Maréchal and Rahner both have tried to show that this is the case. They have done it in slightly different ways that are rather technical and which I shall have to simplify to some extent. Here again the advanced student is referred to their own works.

Maréchal[22] insists on the need of explaining the objectivity of our knowledge as opposed to its immanence. The word 'objectivity' has many possible meanings. Here it means simply the fact of being an "object in consciousness"; the fact of being opposed to the subject, at least in his mind; the fact of being not-I, at least not the knowing I. When a person knows some reality, this reality is somehow in the mind (immanence), but it is in the mind as distinct from it, as opposed to it, as facing it, as an "object." This problem is often overlooked by those who have a rather naive conception of knowledge. They consider the spatial distinction between subject and object sufficient for the objectivity of our knowledge. Animals perceive this spatial distinction, and for sense knowledge as such it seems to be the only "objectivity" available. That is why the knowledge of animals (as far as we can get to know it) is not objective in the strict sense. Animals do not perceive objects as objects; they do not know that what they perceive is not-I. They are, as Scheler has put it, "ecstatically immersed in their environment." That is why they are so perfectly adapted to it and generally so much at a loss outside of it. But that is also why they do not speak and have no culture.

Others explain the objectivity of human knowledge through some kind of awareness of our intellect's passivity with regard to what is known. There is no difficulty in admitting such a passivity in our material senses, but this passivity does not yield more than the spatial objectivity which is present in animal knowledge. It is very difficult to see how our immaterial intellect as such can be passively affected by material objects.

At any rate, Maréchal, along with most of the great philosophers of the past, excludes this explanation. He claims that the object of any intellectual knowledge can be known as object, as not-I, only if the intellect in question either *causes* these objects or actively *strives toward* them. When we cause something or when we strive for it, we know that we are not it, that this thing is not-I; we "live" the objectivity. Except for the so-called "artifacts" humans do not cause the objects of their knowledge. The objectivity of it can therefore be explained only by the fact that the mind strives for these objects, intends them. It can be explained only by the dynamism of the intellect. Thus the dynamism is an a priori condition of the possibility of any object in consciousness. But we have seen that this dynamism coincides with the affirmation of the Infinite. Hence the affirmation of God's existence exerts in human knowledge not only a regulative but also a constitutive function. A person possesses any object only because every time one knows something he is always already beyond it through the infinite openness of his mind. The affirmation of God is not only a psychological necessity (as admitted by Kant) but also a logical necessity. It is not only regulative; it is also constitutive of our knowledge.

Rahner[23] proceeds in a different way, which I hope not to oversimplify by explaining it as follows. Of all objects I get to know, I claim implicitly that they are *something which*. Further characteristics are supplied, which come mostly from sense perception. Thus a dime is *something which* is round, small, made of silver, used as a coin in this country, and so on. Now, whenever we *perceive* (with the senses) in a given individual such a complex totality of sense data, we *conceive* (with the intellect) it at once as universal, as capable of being indefinitely reproduced in other individuals. It is A dime, not THE dime. In other words, we are aware that these data only happen to be embodied in the present individual thing. They might also have been embodied in another one. We call the thing A dime, A being, SOMEthing. This supposes that as soon as we know any reality, we know it only as part of, sharing in, a wider reality. This is true of absolutely all real or conceivable limited reality. Thus the wider reality toward which our intellect transcends whatever we know is one without limits or boundaries, the Unlimited, Infinite Reality. It is only because we have this anticipating grasp of the Absolute, because we preapprehend the Infinite, that we can say of everything we know that it is *some*thing. And it is precisely our power of calling whatever we perceive "something" which transforms our perceptions into concepts, our sensing into thinking. We would have no concepts, no ideas, we would be unable to think and to speak, we would have neither language nor civilization, we would be confined to the animal level of knowing, were it not for the fact that whatever we know is known by us against the Infinite Horizon of Being, of God. Hence the intending of this horizon, the (implicit) affirmation of God, is the a priori condition of the possibility of all human thought and action. It is not only psychologically necessary for humans to affirm God's existence (Kant's transcendental illusion); it is also logically necessary.

After having given extensive attention to the many objections of Kant, I shall now consider more objections coming from present-day philosophers.

F. Contemporary Objections

First let us examine an objection allegedly from Heidegger. He claims that a human being is indeed a dynamism, but one which is a thrust toward nothingness. A human being comprehends the meaning of the word 'not', is able to deny, to negate, hence experiences himself and the other beings as finite only because he is exposed to "nothingness."

In fact what is here presented as an objection rather seems to confirm my position. What the great German philosopher said is not so far removed from what has been explained above. The "nothingness" which is mentioned here is nonbeing. Now as Professor W. Richardson wrote in his work on Heidegger: "Non-being is not Absolute Nothing but Being itself, considered, however, as Other than beings, when beings are taken as the starting point of the consideration."[24]

In English the word 'being' may mean "that which is" and also "that which lets what is be." Being is that through which beings are beings. In German and in a few other languages there are two words for these related but very different ideas. The German calls them respectively *Seiendes* and *Sein*. One way of making this difference clear in English translation is to use the plural form for the former, *beings*, and to speak of the latter as *Being itself*. Another way is to speak of the former as *things* and of the latter as not a thing, as *No-thing*.

This may help us understand what Heidegger meant: man transcends beings toward Being itself, transcends things toward No-thing. Heidegger further claimed that we experience things as things, as finite, only because of this transcending toward No-thing, toward Being itself. We have defended a similar position, although in other terms.

This does not mean, however, that Heidegger agrees with the position defended in this work. The great difference is that whereas I identify Being itself with the infinitely perfect being of God, for Heidegger Being itself is not God. It is difficult and perhaps impossible to say exactly what it is for him, but it is definitely not God. Nevertheless his statement can hardly be presented as an objection against my vindication.

Another objection was presented by my former colleague, Professor Vincent Cooke, S.J.: "You say that there is no real demonstration of God's existence and you criticize the traditional approach, because it passes from the finite to the infinite, from the contingent to the necessary, from the relative to the absolute. Yet you insist that we discover in our experience an undeniable fact which implies that God is possible. Is this undeniable fact not finite, contingent, relative? Do you not use it as the starting point of a real demonstration?"

This clever objection is based on a misunderstanding. It allows me to point out once more the very peculiar nature of the transcendental approach. I do not really "demonstrate" the existence of God. What I do is show that I affirm his existence necessarily and that I have a right to do so. How do I show that I have a right to do so? I point out that he who denies the existence of God explicitly affirms it implicitly. So, this is not a real demonstration, since I already affirm God's existence as soon as I set off to try to "demonstrate" it. Yes, the undeniable fact, my dynamism, is finite, contingent, relative. But I know it as such only by pointing beyond any finiteness, contingency and relativity. I do not pass from this finite, contingent, relative fact to the reality of God. The dynamism is from the start an affirmation of God. There is no passage from nonaffirming to affirming God, but only from implicitly affirming to explicitly affirming the existence of God. Strictly speaking, I use the fact of the dynamism, not as a demonstration, as a starting point, but as that which helps me become aware of what I am always already doing implicitly.

Here is an objection of Antony Flew. After referring to the famous parable of the gardener, presented by John Wisdom, he goes on:

> Sophisticated religious people . . . tend to refuse to allow, not merely that anything actually does occur, but that anything conceivably could occur, which would count against their theological assertions and explanations. But in so far as they do this their supposed explanations are actually vacuous . . . .[25] What would have to occur or to have occurred to constitute for you a disproof of the love, or of the existence of God?[26]

It is true that for the believer as such nothing will ever occur which will make him conclude that God does not exist after all. And rightly so. For by freely making the act of faith he has allowed the mind to fall into the grip of the Absolute himself (that is what faith ultimately consists in), so that there is nothing strange in the fact that even the most baffling occurrences will never upset that faith.

But this is a theological, not a philosophical, answer.

Professor Flew challenges us to apply to our assertion of the existence of God the criterion of falsifiability, which claims that an assertion which cannot be falsified is meaningless. This means that an assertion is meaningless when no actual or possible instance can be mentioned in which it would be false. Thus the assertion that all rivers flow from south to north can be falsified by pointing out the number of rivers which flow in other directions.

Those who claim that unfalsifiable statements are meaningless do not demonstrate this assertion. It is for them an axiom which they gratuitously affirm and which we might as gratuitously deny.

But let us not deny it at once. We might first ask them to apply their test to this statement itself. For if they cannot do this, they will have to admit that the principle of falsifiability is meaningless.

Suppose they give us an instance in which the statement would be falsified. In that case I would try to oblige in my turn by mentioning a case in which the statement that God exists would be falsified. Such a case would occur if somebody were able to demonstrate that the idea of God is contradictory, that an infinitely perfect, necessarily existing being is impossible.

Modern analysts object against our talking of God as a necessary being. Realities, beings, according to them can never be necessary. Only propositions, statements, can be necessary. Thus Professor J. N. Findlay writes: "necessity in propositions merely reflects our use of words, the arbitrary conventions of our language. On such a view the Divine Existence could only be a necessary matter if we had made up our minds to speak theistically whatever the empirical circumstances might turn out to be."[27]

Of course, this objection derives from the philosophy of the analysts, and since it is impossible for me here to explain why I do not accept their philosophy, I cannot give an answer to their objection which might do full justice to it.

Let me rather clearly explain what I mean when I say that God is a necessary Being. I do not mean that he is logically, but I mean that he is ontologically, necessary, that he exists in a necessary way, that he does not merely happen to exist, that he is not a contingent being. God is not logically necessary, but it is logically necessary for me to affirm his existence. I know about God's ontological necessity precisely on account of this logical necessity.

When I say that the affirmation of God's existence is logically necessary, I mean that I would contradict myself if I denied this existence. This contradiction is not explicit; it does not occur between the concepts of my statement. In that sense I am willing to admit that the assertion "God exists" is not logically necessary. It is not analytic, but synthetic a priori. The contradiction occurs between the *content* of my affirmation and the very *activity* by which I assert it. That is why, although I claim that it is logically necessary for me to affirm the existence of God, I prefer not to call this a "demonstration" of his existence.

Professor I. M. Crombie claims in the same vein that all existential propositions are necessarily contingent, "that is to say, it is never true that we can involve ourselves in a breach of the laws of logic by merely denying of something that it exists."[28]

It is true that by denying of something in my experience that it exists I can never be shown to have admitted a contradiction between concepts. Thus if I say, "Words do not exist," or "Language does not exist" or "I do not exist," there is no contradiction between concepts. Neither the concept of "words" nor that of "language" or of "I" implies the concept of existence. Yet there is a contradiction in these denials, one that occurs between content and performance. We might call it a "performative contradiction." It is this kind of contradiction which occurs in the denial of the divine existence. In that sense God is necessary.

G. A Few Characteristics of This Vindication

In this vindication of our right of affirming God's existence we reach God as the ultimate end of the dynamism of our intellect, as the reality which we are always in vain trying to grasp (*Vorgriff*) every time we grasp anything intellectually. The affirmation of this ultimate end is a condition of the possibility of our every act of human knowledge, hence also of our every really human action. God is coaffirmed implicitly in everything we affirm explicitly. He is never really the *object* of our knowledge, but that which makes possible all objects of our knowledge. He is, as Rahner puts it, not the "what," but the "whither" or the "whereunto" of our knowing. We never really know him; we only coknow him, we know him only as the background, the horizon of all our knowledge. We see him never directly, but only, as it were, out of the corner of our eye. If, when espying him in this indirect way, we turn our gaze upon him to see him more clearly, what we perceive is no longer him, but an object, that is, an idol. In this sense it is true that the dynamism of our intellect aims at nothingness. What I intend in all my knowledge is not a thing, no-thing, since it is the condition of the possibility of all things in my knowledge.

Yet we speak and we think of God. When we do, we turn him to some extent into an object, a thing, and we transcend even him, as put in our words or conceived in our mind, toward our whereunto. Whenever we speak or think of God we make him finite, but we are aware that by doing this we are wrong.

The great scholastic philosophers of the past were quite aware of this state of affairs. That is why they insisted on the difference between what we know and the manner of our knowing it. What we know, so they said, is correct, but our manner of knowing it is not. Or, again, we both represent and mean God. We cannot mean, intend or affirm him without also representing him, picturing him somehow in our mind, because our intellectual knowledge is always accompanied by sense knowledge. The picture, the representation, is always defective, but what we mean or intend is true. This may have been what Wittgenstein had in mind when he wrote: "There is indeed the inexpressible. This shows itself. It is the mystical" (*Tract.* 6.522). This is also why traditional philosophy insists so much on the doctrine of analogy, which we shall consider later in this book.

It is easy to understand why this transcendental approach does not bother much with Hume's and Kant's attacks against the principle of causality. These attacks were aimed at the principle of efficient causality, which I do not use in my approach. Instead I use the principle of intelligibility, as "exercised" in the dynamism of my intellect, in my "pure desire to know" (Lonergan). I reach God, not as the first cause of all things, but as the condition of their intelligibility. I have used, not the metaphysics of being, but the metaphysics of the knowledge of being. My approach is not ontic, but ontological.

As applied to the present context, the principle of intelligibility is also known as the principle of sufficient reason, or the principle of the foundation of being. Whatever is has a sufficient reason for its existence. Whatever is not intelligible by itself is intelligible only by being referred to that which is intelligible by itself. Whatever is is on account of something. The very fact that we are aware of the finiteness of whatever we know implies that no object of our experience is intelligible by itself. Every one of them needs a complement of intelligibility. We LIVE this complement through the dynamism of our intellect. We make it explicit when we assert God as the source of all intelligibility.

Should we not demonstrate the principle of intelligibility before using it? It cannot be "demonstrated" any more than the existence of God, and for the same reason. We would be using it in the very attempt of demonstrating it. It can only be vindicated, as we vindicate our right of affirming God's existence.

Practically the two vindications coincide. We LIVE the principle and the affirmation before we can express them in words. They are our intellect in act, what scholastic philosophy called our "agent intellect." Our only way of establishing their validity is to try to show that those who deny them in words use them in fact, in their knowledge and their action. We must use "retortion" and show that, like the existence of God, the principle of intelligibility may be denied only through an affirmation which asserts it implicitly.

Let me finally draw attention upon the fact that this vindication does not make us "arrive" at God. We do not discover the reality of God by starting from the reality of the objects of our experience, although without such objects we would never become aware of his existence. I have mentioned above the serious objections which may be raised against any attempt at arriving at God while starting from creatures. How can we ever hope to pass from the finite to the infinite, from the relative to the absolute, from the contingent to the necessary? How can the conclusion be stronger than the premises? How can we ever hope to bridge the infinite gap between God and the things of our experience? The fact is that we do not have to bridge it; we do not really arrive at God. We start with him; we are with him from the beginning. He is already in our mind when we know our first object, when we make our first affirmation, since only he makes them possible for us. We reach God at once or never at all. In this sense every attempt at a demonstration of God's existence "begs the question," is engaged in a "circle." However, this is not a vicious circle; it is the most conspicuous instance of that "circuminsession" of all the great metaphysical truths, which makes metaphysics both so very simple and so very difficult, and which explains why, of its very nature, it lies beyond the grasp of a purely analytical approach. Augustine and Pascal had grasped this basic way in which our mind knows God when they present him as telling us:

"You would not be looking for me if you had not already found me."

H. Summarizing the Vindication

Our vindication might be summarized in the following syllogism:

If the infinitely perfect being is possible, it exists.
But the infinitely perfect being is possible.
Therefore the infinitely perfect being exists.

The major is evident as soon as one understands it.

The minor must be demonstrated. We do it by means of the dynamism of our intellect. Whatever reality we know, we know as limited. But to know a limit as limit means to be, in fact or in striving, beyond this limit. Hence our mind keeps striving beyond any limited reality toward the unlimited reality, the infinitely perfect reality. This implies at least that the infinitely perfect reality is possible. Otherwise the mind of man would be congenitally the faculty of the impossible. Both Kant and Hegel claimed that every "demonstration" of God's existence contained the ontological argument, Kant disapprovingly and Hegel approvingly. What we have said shows in what sense this is true. Only the basic weakness of the ontological argument has been eliminated: the fact that it tries to pass from concepts to reality. Here the passage occurs from the undeniable fact of the striving of the intellect to the undeniable fact of the existence of the All-Perfect. And this passage is a transition, not from not-knowing to knowing, but from knowing implicitly to knowing explicitly.

Another way of showing this starts with the remark of Descartes and of Kant that we naturally get the idea of an infinitely perfect being. Many people deny that such a being exists. But is it not contradictory to deny that the infinitely perfect being exists? Does such a being not possess the basic perfection of "being"? Or, if we wish to prevent Kant's objection, that of "necessary being"?

Yet this is not a valid proof of God's existence. A distinction must be made. There is a contradiction in the statement "the infinitely perfect being does not exist." But this contradiction may reside either in its subject (the infinitely perfect being) or in the statement itself (between its subject and its predicate). In the former hypothesis the statement is true; in the latter one the statement is false.

Thus in the statement "female fathers do not exist" there is a contradiction in the subject of the statement, and the statement is true. Whereas in the statement "horses are free agents" the contradiction lies in the statement itself, between its subject and its predicate. And the statement is false.

The ontological argument takes for granted that there is no contradiction in the subject of our statement, that the concept "the infinitely perfect being" is not contradictory. We have no right to do this. We must first establish this. That is what we have done through our intellect's dynamism. Then indeed the contradiction resides in the statement itself. It is contradictory to say that the infinitely perfect being (once its noncontradiction, its possibility, has been established) does not exist.[29]

We might even further summarize our way of arguing in this simple way. Our basic existential affirmations, the ones through which we affirm the reality of something, have implicitly this form: THIS IS. THIS stands for a reality which we designate through its essence; in that sense THIS stands for the essence, the whatness, the limitation. IS stands for the existence, the thatness, the reality. Of itself IS has no limits. Should there be a limit, of that limit, too, we would have to say that it IS.

Our mind keeps yearning for some essence, some whatness, which is as wide as its basic predicate (IS), of which we
might say without any restriction, any limitation, THIS IS. It
keeps pointing toward a reality whose essence coincides with its
existence, whose nature it is TO BE. This reality is God, Being
Itself.

3. Blondel's Demonstration of the Existence of God[1]

THE MOST TYPICAL FEATURE of the vindication submitted in the last chapter, that which differentiates it most from the traditional "proofs," is the use of the transcendental method. As applied to the central part of philosophy, to metaphysics, this approach claims that the implicit affirmation of all the great metaphysical verities, including the existence of God, is a condition of the possibility of all human knowledge. These verities are not gathered from sense experience, as it is claimed by all empiricists, including the dogmatic empiricists.[2] They are virtually inborn in us. No human experience is purely sense experience. All our sense experience is in fact carried by an intellectual skeleton which consists of metaphysical affirmations. Metaphysics becomes explicit in the experience into which the intellect projects it.

Metaphysics is the a priori condition not only of all human thought but also of all human willing and action. Although I have not insisted on this aspect, it is implied in my position, since every human volition and action presupposes some intellectual knowledge, an at least implicit affirmation.

That human action implies all the basic affirmations of metaphysics, including the affirmation of the existence of God, has been shown in a different way by Maurice Blondel (1861–1949) in his great book *L'Action* (1893). Although he

93

rarely uses the word, Blondel handles the transcendental method with great skill.

Blondel's main insight might be summarized as follows: Man's willed will never comes up to his willing will. The "willed will" is an act of willing, a volition. Whenever we will something, there is in us something that wills and an act of willing. We are rather clearly aware of the act of willing, but we hardly advert to that which wills in us. In the terminology of Stephan Strasser[3] the act of willing is a "quasi-object" in me. It is not an object distinct from me; it is something in me, something which is more intimate to me than an arm or an eye. Yet it is not I. I do not coincide totally with it; it stands somewhere between an ordinary object and the pure subject, hence the term 'quasi-object'. The willing will, on the other hand, coincides with the subject; it is I, the primordial, originating subject as willing. We speak of it as if it were an object or a quasi-object, because we can only think and speak of realities by turning them into some kind of object. But in so doing we create a false image of it, in the same way in which we create a false image of our pure Ego, of our I as pure subject, whenever we speak or think of it, by making an object out of it. Our innermost subjectivity is beyond the reach of our consciousness. It is supraconscious. We live, we think, we will, we love, we freely decide out of it, we cannot directly know it in its primordial purity.

The pure Ego as thinking may be called "thinking thought," as opposed to our "thought thoughts," our ideas. It is the intellect in its dynamism. The pure Ego as willing is the willing will, as opposed to the willed will, our everyday volitions.

Maréchal and transcendental Thomism have concentrated their attention on thinking thought and insist less on the willing will. It would be an exaggeration, however, to claim that they have wholly neglected it. Maréchal's intellectual dynamism implies a striving; it refers not only to the intellect but also to the will. We may equate the dynamism of the intellect with thinking thought as long as we remember that thinking is an activity, that dynamism is a striving, that therefore it also involves the will. In other words, the distinction between thinking thought and willing will is far from complete. These two basic aspects of the Pure Ego imply each other. They are complementary; it is not possible to study one without the other. That is why Maréchal devotes a whole section of Cahier V to a study of the relation between intellect and will.[4] And that is why Blondel writes that action is "a synthesis of willing, knowing and being . . . the precise point where the worlds of thought, of morality and of science converge" (28). And again, "Thought is a form of action, which it transforms into a free volition" (119).

It is not surprising then that there are great similarities between the two thinkers. Both investigate the activities of the Pure I; both reach the conclusion that these activities reach all the way up to the Infinite, the Transcendent. Both start from an undeniable fact of daily experience: Maréchal from the fact that we affirm, Blondel from the fact that we act. Both establish the absolute value of metaphysics and show that man is made for something which he cannot reach by his own devices.

But there are also considerable differences between the two approaches. Maréchal uses the road of thought; Blondel, that of action. As a result, although both works are long and, at times, quite difficult to follow, it is easier to summarize Maréchal than Blondel, since it is easier to grasp our intellectual life intellectually than to do so with our action. But what Maréchal wins thus in clarity and conciseness, he loses in warmth and existential concreteness. Blondel is nearer to real life, with its activity, its love, its feelings and emotions.

Maréchal, whose work bears the title *The Starting Point of Metaphysics,* is more useful if we wish to establish the absolute value of metaphysics. Blondel, whose work bears the subtitle *Attempt at a Critique of Life and of a Science of Action,* treats of metaphysics only in passing, but time and again he has pages of great depth and beauty. Both establish that God exists. This is not the main purpose of their work; it is an undeniable truth that they discover to be implied in their starting point. Both of them show that human beings are made for a union with God which they can never hope to reach by their own means. While Maréchal insists little on this problem, Blondel devotes many pages of his book to it.

Maréchal arrives at God as the Illimited, the Infinite, for which the human intellect keeps striving, as it is shown by the fact that the intellect is aware of the limited nature of every object it knows. He arrives at the idea of the supernatural somewhat in the same way: the human person is aware that every way of knowing God which falls short of a real intuition is a limited kind of knowledge. Therefore there is something in him which is beyond it, which keeps craving for this intuitive vision. From this he concludes that such an intuitive vision cannot be contradictory, that it is possible.

Blondel arrives first at the supernatural, not the christian supernatural, but some undifferentiated supernatural. His work primarily intends, not to demonstrate the existence of God, but to show that the supernatural is indispensable for a person's action, although one is unable to reach it by one's own means.

With Maréchal's approach it is not too difficult to arrive at God rather rapidly. Since our dynamism strives beyond any limit, it strives for the unlimited. Hence this unlimited is not contradictory; it is possible, and therefore it exists. Blondel does not use the idea of the limit known as such. But he too insists on a dynamism, the dynamism of the will. To an objection that inquired whether the starting point of his research and that which predetermined its result was not "willing the infinite," Blondel answered that this willing of the infinite was not the starting point but the final outcome of philosophical research. True, from the start the thought occurred to him that this might be the real principle of human activity, but he tried to shake off this hypothesis, to find other possible explanations, and it was only when he found himself forced to give up all other possibilities that he accepted the idea that it is indeed this striving of the human will for infinity which animates the whole of human life.[5]

That is why Blondel's itinerary is long and tortuous. When science wishes to explain a fact, it considers a certain number of hypothetical solutions and eliminates all those which can be eliminated until it discovers one which can no longer be discarded. Blondel calls his own approach "scientific." His science of action may overlook no possible explanation; it must try out all possible solutions.

> We must welcome all the denials that destroy each other, as if it were possible to admit all of them together; we must enter into all the prejudices, as if they were legitimate; into all the errors, as if they were sincere; into all the passions, as if they possessed the generosity of which they boast; into all the philosophical systems as if each one of them encompassed the infinite truth it believes it has discovered. We must assume into ourselves all consciences, become the intimate accomplices of all of them, so as to find out whether they carry within themselves their justification. Let them be their own referees; let them see whither their most sincere and intimate will would lead them; let them learn what they do without knowing it, and what they know already without willing it and without doing it.[6]

In this laborious way Blondel arrives at the following conclusion: *The natural order is insufficient.* The "natural order" he speaks of is not that of the theologians, but that of the naturalistic philosophers, the order of sense experience, of human natural activities. It is one which includes no relation to God. So when Blondel asserts that the natural order is not sufficient, he means that there is more to life and to reality than what meets the eye. The human person must acknowledge a dependence on a higher being and try to find out more about this being and how one should relate to it. If the natural order is not sufficient, the human person must look for a supernatural order. Blondel reaches the idea of the supernatural order as a philosopher, by using only reason and without any help of religion or revelation. He shows that we act reasonably by looking for such an order, by accepting it if it is presented to us, by doing what is required of us if we are to enter it. This supernatural order, which seems to come wholly from without, is thus, in fact, to a great extent craved for from within. It seems to threaten our freedom, our autonomy. In reality it is demanded by them, so that what is willed by us may come up to that which wills in us.

> Let no one misunderstand the strictly philosophical purpose that inspires this inquiry: it always revolves around this same thought: "How to bring the term willed up to the level of the very principle of the voluntary aspiration?" For one cannot lead men to submission save by making them understand that it is the secret of their true independence. So, it is necessary to aim at true independence in order to understand the secret of the necessary submission. Moreover, even when it is a question of the supernatural, we have to do with a preoccupation that is profoundly human and rather like a cry of nature that makes itself heard. It is a question of seeing how this notion of the supernatural seems necessary for the human will so that the equation of action may be established in consciousness. It is not a question of determining the actual content of divine revelation . . . The role of the philosopher is to make sure that, fully consistent with our secret desire, we move even to the plane of literal practice; his task is to express the inevitable exigencies of thought and a kind of natural prayer of the human will. Nothing more, but nothing less.[7]

At this stage Blondel's supernatural is not yet the christian supernatural, the one known through revelation. It is an undetermined supernatural. Reason knows very little about its content, about its exigencies. It knows, however, that whatever this content and these exigencies may be, the human person will have to accept them if the willed will is to come up to the willing will.

There is, however, one very important element of this supernatural which reason knows: the existence of a supreme Being on whom we depend. Blondel calls this being the *unique necessary*. It is not reached deductively, by some kind of formal-logical reasoning; it is implied in the very thrust of our voluntary activity. Logical arguments do not fully satisfy in this domain. Much better is the proof which is carried by the whole of our life. We may try to present it in intellectual terms. But that will be possible only if, says Blondel, we combine the various traditional arguments for God's existence, none of which is sufficient by itself, whereas, taken together, they tend to coincide with our vital dynamism and offer a real demonstration.

Thus take the proof from contingency. Whatever we may know or achieve or reach looks insufficient and limited to us. It is not nothing, but it is not enough either. Which goes to show that we will the objects of our everyday endeavors only because our will always already reaches beyond them. Understood in this way, the argument from contingency, "instead of looking for the necessary outside of the contingent, as a further term, shows it in the contingent itself, as a reality that is already present."[8]

About the teleological argument Blondel writes, "Thus the order, the harmony, the wisdom that I discover in myself and in things is not merely an effect from which some reasoning would force me to rise toward a cause which is absent from its work; I may not consider this harmony and this beauty as constituted and subsisting in itself; I do not make of it the premises of a deduction; I do not use a principle of causality; but I find in this imperfect wisdom of things and of my thought the necessary presence and action of a perfect thought and power."[9]

Finally Blondel comments as follows on the *ontological argument*: The idea of the perfect is not a fiction of our mind, but rather

> a reality that is wholly alive in our consciousness which derives from our total action all the positive certitude which is already in us. It is for us not so much a view as a life (*moins une vue qu' une vie*). It does not result from a speculation; it is tied to the whole movement of thought and of action. It is not some abstraction, from which one might only derive an abstraction, but an act that makes us act. It is not some ideal from which one would claim to extract the real but a real in which one finds the ideal. . . .
>
> That is why it is legitimate here, and only here, to identify idea and being, because under this abstract identity we put first that of thought and action. We should therefore not simply say that we pass from the idea to the being; we must say that we first find the idea in the being and the being in action. . . . To reach the "unique necessary" we do not grasp it in itself where we are not; but we start from it in us, where it is, in order better to see that it is by understanding to some extent what it is. We are forced to affirm it to the extent that we have the idea of it, because this idea itself is a reality.[10]

Blondel considers these arguments solid, but he knows that they do not force the human mind to accept their conclusion. Only in mathematics, and to some extent in science, can a conclusion force itself upon us. In all the great "mysteries" of life man may refuse assent. He assents freely; he makes the option to assent.

> Yes or no, is (man) going to will to live, even to the point of dying from it, if one may speak this way, by consenting to be supplanted by God? Or will he pretend to suffice without him, profiting by his necessary presence without making it voluntary, borrowing from him the strength to get along without him and willing infinitely without willing the infinite? . . . Not that this

tragic opposition is revealed to all with this precision and rigor. But if the thought that there is something to be done with life is offered to all, this is enough to indicate that even the most obtuse are also called to resolve the question of the great affair, the unique necessary.[11]

This strange text ("even to the point of dying from it . . . to be supplanted by God") prepares the way for a surprising distinction which Blondel makes at this point between the *existence* and the *being* of God.

According to Blondel "Every system that insists on putting being at the end of some theoretical research will finally fail in its affirmations. For the fullness of being resides precisely in that which separates the abstract idea from the act out of which it is born and from the act toward which its only function is to orient us."[12]

And again, "It is not merely by *seeing,* but by *living* that we advance into being as we perform, as it were, a leap of generosity beyond the reach of intellectual justifications. To possess is more than to affirm, but one affirms better only by possessing more: we cannot have a better intellectual grasp of being without grasping it more solidly in our acts."[13]

These passages taken from another work of Blondel help us to understand him when he writes: "While showing that this conception, necessarily engendered in consciousness, forces us to affirm at least implicitly the living reality of this infinite perfection, there was no question of concluding from it the being of God. We simply realized that this necessary idea of the real God leads us to the supreme alternative on which it will depend whether God really is or is not for us."[14]

In other words, Blondel makes a distinction between our knowledge of the existence and our knowledge of the being of God. The knowledge of God's existence is implied in the thrust of our willing will. It is not free and it implies no option; it is given with human nature. On the other hand, we know about the *being* of God only when we consciously and freely admit that God exists and when we live up to this fundamental truth.

Then God not only exists but he also is, is for us, is our God. Then we reach not only his existence but also his being. Every human person necessarily and unconsciously admits the existence of God. Only those who freely and consciously welcome this "lived" affirmation and live up to it reach the being of God.

Thus we see how for Blondel theory is not enough; action is required along with a certain amount of "passion," of suffering. The idea of God must have an influence upon our life if we wish to make this idea come alive and lead us not only to the existence but to the being of God.

> The thought of God in us depends doubly on our action. On the one hand, it is because, in acting, we discover an infinite disproportion in ourselves that we are constrained to seek the equation between our action and the infinite. On the other hand, it is because, in affirming absolute perfection, we never succeed in equating our own affirmation, that we are obliged to seek its complement and commentary in action. The problem is brought up by action and only action can solve it.
>
> As soon as we believe that we know God well enough, we no longer know him. We might say that the moment of his apparition in consciousness looks so much like eternity that we are as it were afraid of entering into it entirely, with our eyes turned toward the lightning that has flashed only to make the night even darker. But the mixture of shadow and light remains such that the presumption of those who believe that they see and the claim of those who make believe that they do not know are both confounded: against those who see too clearly we must hold that, in what we know and will, God remains that which we can neither know nor do; against those who are voluntarily blind we must hold that, without any dialectical complication nor length of studies, in a trice, for everyone, at all times, God is the immediate certitude without which there is no other, the primordial light, the language we know without having learned

it. He is the only one whom we cannot look for in vain, yet we can never find him fully. . . .

Thus, at the very moment when we seem to touch God by a stroke of thought, he escapes if we do not keep him, if we do not seek him through action. His immobility can be aimed at as a steady target only by a perpetual movement. Wherever we stop, he is not; wherever we keep marching, he is. We must always proceed beyond, because he is always further. The moment we no longer stand in awe, as before an ineffable newness, but look upon him from the outside as an object of knowledge, or a simple occasion for speculative study, without a young heart and an aching love, the game is over; we have in our hands nothing more than a phantom and an idol. Whatever we have seen or felt about him is but a means for going further; it is a road; hence we do not stop on it, otherwise it no longer is a road. Thinking of God is an action; we never act without cooperating with him and without making him collaborate with us. . . . And it is because action is a synthesis of man with God that it is in perpetual becoming, as if under the sway of a yearning for infinite growth .[15]

But action is not enough to reach our end. A certain amount of passivity, of accepted, and therefore active, passivity is also required. "Action cannot shut itself up in the natural order. . . . Yet, by itself, it cannot get beyond it. Its life lies beyond its own power. . . . In order to reestablish in his willed action the fullness of its original nature, must man not allow the First Cause to take up again the first place? Man must yield. That which he does not kill in himself kills him, and his own will prevents him from reaching his real will."[16]

Here is the place of giving up, of sacrifice, abnegation, mortification, suffering and pain. It changes us for better or for worse; it crushes us or makes us grow. It prevents us from settling down as if we had already reached what we are made for.

Between authentic love and active suffering there exists a reciprocity, and, as it were, an identity. . . . To love means to love suffering, because it means to love the joy and the action of the other in us. . . . If we understand well that pain and suffering bring about infinite and real joy, have we not solved the supreme difficulty of life and removed the main stumbling block for human consciousness, by finally giving our will the great relief of being able to ratify everything?[17] . . . Mortification is the real metaphysical experimentation, done on being itself. That which dies is that which prevents us from seeing, from acting, from living. That which survives is already that which is born anew. . . . Nobody loves God without suffering; nobody sees God without dying. Nothing reaches him that is not risen from death: no will is good if it has not moved out of itself, wholly to make room for the total invasion of his will.[18]

4. Knowledge of God and the Supernatural[1]

AFTER HAVING EXPLAINED some of Blondel's views about the existence of God, I would like to take up an objection against Maréchal's approach to this problem. It shows the great similarity that exists in many respects between the ideas of the two philosophers.

We have shown that the human mind keeps striving for an infinite reality. The person knows it very imperfectly, only by intending it, by striving for it. What kind of knowledge of this reality, of God, does one basically yearn for? There can be no doubt about the answer: for a perfect kind of knowledge, that is, for a direct intuitive knowledge of God, since about every other kind of knowledge one is at once aware that it is imperfect, limited, restricted, which implies that something in him strives past it.

But finite man is unable to reach an intuitive knowledge of the infinite being. This knowledge is known in christian theology as the *beatific vision*: it belongs to the domain of the strictly supernatural. Many philosophers have objected that Maréchal's approach to God brings in theological considerations and involves the supernatural.

It does, but only to the extent that the supernatural is conceivable by reason. Before explaining this, let me mention once more the important distinction we must make in speaking of the 'supernatural'. This term may be taken in a wider or in a

105

stricter sense. In the wider sense it means that which is above nature, where nature is understood as that which is perceptible by the senses, which we meet in our ordinary everyday experience. This is the supernatural rejected by all naturalistic philosophers. It includes realities such as God and the soul. Spiritualistic philosophers generally refuse to call such realities supernatural because they are knowable by human reason.

Supernatural in the stricter sense, as understood by the christian theologians, means that which is in itself unreachable and unknowable by the human mind, that which is a pure gratuitous gift of God to human beings. It includes what theologians call the beatific vision, sanctifying grace, the theological virtues of faith, hope and charity.

Now to the above objection (that we make the value of human knowledge dependent on such realities, which lie beyond the scope of philosophy) I answer with Maréchal that this supernatural in the stricter sense is not totally beyond the reach of philosophy. Human reason can know it, to some extent, as a *possible* reality. We have already started to show that philosophy can establish that one of them is a possible, that is, not a contradictory reality: the intuitive vision of God. Since we know God through reason, as shown by our previous vindication, since we are clearly aware that our knowledge of him is limited, since we see at once that every knowledge of him which is not intuitive, which is not a direct seeing with the mind's eye of his divine nature, is limited and restricted, something in us still keeps striving for such an intuition. And this implies that such an intuitive vision is not contradictory, that it is possible.

Our will also strives for intuitive knowledge. Whoever admits that this kind of knowledge is better, more desirable than the knowledge we can reach through reasoning, has implicitly admitted that something in one is yearning for such a knowledge. The most arduous problem of ethics, the philosophy of human action, is to find out what is the final purpose of human activity, of human life. What does the human person ultimately exist for? Reason finds it very difficult, if not impossible, to answer this most essential question. It is no wonder that this problem is involved in darkness, since the above considerations make us aware that it leads us straight into the strictly supernatural. It seems hard to deny that the purpose of human life is that for which its innermost being keeps striving. This is the intuitive vision of the Infinite Being.

The question might be raised why, if these considerations lie within the purview of reason (and not only of religious faith, as some will object), other philosophers, especially those who have not been influenced by christianity, have never suspected these possibilities. Is it true that none of them have? Not to speak of the many Far Eastern philosophers with their strong mystical bent, would anybody deny that Plotinus knew of them? And what are we to make of the following words of Aristotle?

> But such a life (a life of contemplation) would be too high for man; for it is not in so far as he is man that he will live so, but in so far as something divine is present in him; and by so much as this is superior to our composite nature is its activity superior to that which is the exercise of the other kind of virtue. If reason is divine, then, in comparison with man, the life according to it is divine in comparison with human life.[2]

Philosophy as such may even go somewhat further in this line. If man is forced by his very nature to envisage the possibility and the desirability of something which lies above it, if he keeps striving for something which he cannot reach by his own devices, he owes it to himself to look out and inquire whether the Infinite for which he cannot help striving has not spoken in history and, as it were, extended a helping hand and enabled man to know and to reach, with his help, that which he craves for and is unable to reach unaided. Christians claim that the Infinite has indeed spoken in history. Philosophy as such demands that every human person should examine these claims and, if they turn out to be right, heed the invitation of the Absolute.[3]

Here is where philosophy as such finds a place in human life for a possible extra knowledge which man may receive from "outside," although he yearns for it from "inside" (faith), for a possible extra power (sanctifying grace) which may enable man to reach what he is made for and is unable to reach by himself.

Every philosophical system owes it to itself to discuss these all-important problems of human destiny. Quite a number do not, especially nowadays. Some of them content themselves with presenting the different systems of philosophy that have been constructed throughout the ages. For them philosophy is nothing but the history of philosophy. They seem unaware of the fact that if all philosophers had followed their way of philosophizing, there would be no philosophy! Others are unwilling to tackle the basic problems of human destiny and to construct all-embracing systems of reality. They concentrate their efforts on small, special problems. But such small problems are always studied and solved by them in function of an unconscious, comprehensive, all-embracing philosophy which they are unwilling or unable to render explicit. Their philosophical constructions look like a regiment with unprotected flanks.

Most great philosophers of the past and many contemporary philosophers have tried and still try to build comprehensive views of reality. In connection with the problem which occupies us here three attitudes are possible: atheism, pantheism and theism.

Atheists deny the existence of God. They pay no attention to man's awareness of the limitation of everything in the universe, or they explain it away.

The pantheists (in the strict sense) admit that there is an infinite being, but they equate him with the totality of the real.

They solve the difficult problem of the relation between the human person and God by practically suppressing one of the elements of it, by making of the person a mode of the Absolute, a wave in the ocean of divinity. Their system is very attractive, because it looks like a nicely finished construction, a powerful dome of which the Absolute is the keystone. Unfortunately, because it is the keystone, the Absolute is no longer transcendent; it has become part of the structure and has been relativized. And in the process the human being has lost autonomy.

Therefore the best solution seems to be the theistic one. It too looks like a dome, a cupola. But the keystone is replaced by a large, gaping aperture opening upon infinity. At the end of one's efforts the theistic philosopher concludes: There should be more, yet I can no longer continue. And since he knows that there is more, and that there exists a being who can tell him about this more, he feels that he owes it to his own highly cherished autonomy to listen to this being. This conclusion may be summarized in the words of K. Rahner: Man is the being who in history must listen to a possible communication of the Absolute.

Catholics—and many other christians—believe that they have become partakers of God's own nature through sanctifying grace. God, as Rahner puts it, has become the quasi-formal cause of their very being. He is no longer only their maker, causing them to share being; he is also their Father, making them share his own divine nature. This is a purely gratuitous gift not demanded by human nature. The human person is human even without it. Nevertheless there is something in human nature which vaguely yearns for this gift. This becomes evident if we reflect that this "divinization" is "good" for man. Something is good for a being only when this being wishes to have it, craves it, desires it.

Catholic theology has always admitted that there is in the

human being an *obediential potency* for divinization, that is, a capability for it which cannot be actualized by the person or by any finite agency. But this obediential potency may be interpreted in two ways: (1) as a mere possibility, as meaning only that it is not contradictory for a human being to be divinized. Those who hold this position are known as *extrinsicists*; for them the divine munificence comes wholly from without, and there is in humans not even a slight desire for it. It is somewhat like a lump of gold in one's stomach. It is no contradiction to say that there is gold in my stomach, but my stomach does not have the slightest appetite for gold. Obediential potency can also be viewed: (2) as a vague desire, a craving, a yearning for an enrichment of our being, the nature of which we do not comprehend, the fulfillment of which we cannot reach by our own means. That which we have explained above makes it clear that this second interpretation is to be preferred.

But there is a serious objection to it. If God has made human beings with such a desire, does God not owe it to himself to fulfill this desire? Then sanctifying grace is no longer a gratuitous gift; it is due to human nature. And this contradicts a basic teaching of catholic doctrine. It does away with the distinction between nature and the supernatural in the strict sense. Maréchal desired to maintain this distinction, and that is why he affirmed that the dynamism of the intellect implies nothing more than this: the created intellect, by its own nature, is capable of being raised to the vision of the divine essence. Even an extrinsicist might admit this. Is there not something more?

In order to avoid both extrinsicism and the denial of the gratuitousness of divinization, Rahner has introduced the notion of the "supernatural existential." The term 'existential' is borrowed from the philosophy of Heidegger. It means a permanent disposition of the person, previous to any free decision. Rahner's "supernatural existential" consists in the fact that, previous to any free decision, every human person is invited by God to accept divinization freely. It is *a standing invitation to accept divinization*. We know from revelation that God wishes all persons to be saved. This divine will produces an effect in humans: the supernatural existential. This existential is not part of human nature, but it is given to every human being in the present order of the world. Thus, for Rahner the human state of "pure nature" does not exist and has never existed. It is a *Restbegriff* (a residual concept), that which remains when from a person's nature as it exists today we subtract the supernatural existential. In this way Rahner is able to maintain both the gratuitous character of the supernatural and the fact that there is in human beings a yearning for it, and thus to exclude extrinsicism.

But if the yearning of human beings for the supernatural is to be explained by the supernatural existential, and if this is added to human nature by God, are we not then back in extrinsicism? Where is the place of the intellectual dynamism in all of this? The supernatural existential, God's salvific will, the standing invitation addressed to all human beings to accept divinization, is *good* for a person. This means that something in a human being desires it, yearns for it. This yearning coincides with the dynamism of his intellect and of his will.

I have mentioned the necessity of an option for those who will accept my vindication. This might easily be misunderstood, as if this vindication had no solid foundation in reason, were simply a matter of the heart. It seems to contradict what I have been emphasizing above: that the human intellect necessarily affirms God; what Blondel shows in his work: that the human will necessarily wills God. How can such a necessity be reconciled with the need for an option?

Blondel answers by making a distinction between God's existence (which is necessarily affirmed and willed by us) and God's being (which is not reached without an option). I have put it differently by saying that the unconscious and therefore unfree affirmation of God occurs necessarily (it coincides with our dynamism), but that the conscious and free affirmation is up to each one of us. Or again we might say: Our thinking thought and our willing will cannot help affirming and loving God. It is not so, however, for our thought thought and our willed will. And as long as they have not turned toward God, he is not yet *our God*.

Blondel has studied the effects of the option upon our knowledge of God. He writes: "Knowledge, which before the option was simply subjective and propulsive, becomes after the option privative and constitutive of being"[4]: *privative of being* in those who make a negative option; *constitutive of being* for those who opt positively. In what sense is a negative option *privative of being*? Blondel's *L'Action* is an answer to this question. He himself has briefly summarized the whole book as follows:

> To believe that one can reach being and legitimately affirm any reality whatsoever without having reached the very end of the series that goes from the first sense intuition to the necessity of God and of religious practice, is to remain in an illusion: One cannot stop at an intermediate object and make an absolute truth of it without falling into the idolatry of the understanding.[5]

That an option is required to reach the conscious affirmation of God is well illustrated by the following remark of a noted philosopher: "I have met philosophers who have said that, if I could show them that the existence of God followed from the fact that contradictories are always false, they would abandon their belief that the latter is a fact."[6]

We should keep in mind that an option is performed by the will, not by the intellect. It happens frequently in our times that the option is affirmative, that the person *as willing* pays allegiance to the Absolute without the same person, *as thinking*, being able to translate this into intellectual language. This person's Absolute may be art, truth, human progress, the

welfare of mankind. As long as one does not make *oneself* into
the Absolute, the option is positive and right and that person is
an "anonymous theist."

An option is an act of the will; it is a free choice. As
christians we know that in the present supernaturalized order of
the world every free choice of the human person is influenced
not only by God's creative influx (as known by reason) but also
by his divinizing grace (as known by faith). This therefore
applies also to the option of which we are speaking here.
Nobody can make this positive option without the help of God's
grace.[7] To make it is a meritorious act: it is the first step toward
accepting the standing invitation to divinization. It is not only
an acknowledgment of the God of nature but also a step toward
acknowledgment of the God of grace.

Blondel was thinking of this when he wrote, "It is not only
the living man who lives in every philosopher; it is philosophy
itself that is and that will always naturally, normally be 'one
who prays' ('une orante')."[8] Or again there is another saying
which he liked so much,

> Sacrifice is the solution of the metaphysical problem
> through the experimental method. And if, throughout the course
> of its development, action has turned out to be a new source of
> light, it is also necessary that at the very outcome the knowledge
> which follows upon the perfect act of abnegation should contain
> a fuller knowledge of being. It no longer sees it from without; it
> has grasped it, it possesses it, it discovers being in itself:
> *authentic philosophy is the holiness of reason.*[9]

5. Can God's Existence Be Demonstrated Scientifically?

BEFORE WE CAN ANSWER this question, we must remember what is meant by science. Science may mean, in its widest sense, any organized body of knowledge. In this sense of the word not only history and geography but also philosophy and theology may be called sciences. Now, it is quite evident that, each in its own peculiar way, theology and philosophy can lead us to some knowledge of God.

Science, in its strictest sense, which is also its everyday sense, refers to the experimental sciences. It is an organized body of knowledge derived from measurements, quantification, experimentation, based on the hypothesis of universal determinism, enabling its practicioners to predict future events. In that sense of the word 'science' the answer to the above question must be NO.

This kind of science studies antecedents and consequents or constructs models that apply to the world of phenomena. God is neither an antecedent nor a consequent; he is not a model and he does not become visible in the world of phenomena.

Science is concerned with facts, laws, hypotheses and theories. A fact is a connection between phenomena. This lump of lead melts at 327.5 centigrade. A law is a statement about constant relations between phenomena. Lead melts at 327.5 C. God is neither a fact nor a law. A hypothesis is a tentative explanation suggested in order to explain laws and facts. Might

114

God not be used as a hypothesis? God is not a scientific hypothesis, because from such hypothesis it must be possible to deduce certain conclusions that may be experimentally verified. From the hypothesis "God" nothing can be deduced which may be thus verified. Therefore God is not a scientific hypothesis. A theory is a synthesis of laws and hypotheses covering a broad field of phenomena. Since God is not a law or a hypothesis, he cannot be a theory either. The conclusion is that if we take the word 'science' in its usual strict sense, science cannot establish the existence of God. On the other hand, since science moves on the level of phenomena and since God transcends this level, no scientific objection against God's existence can have the slightest value.

I have briefly explained above how metaphysics may be considered the animating principle, the "soul" of all our knowledge, everyday and scientific knowledge alike. This entails that in scientific work the scientist continually uses the basic metaphysical principles that are virtually inborn to the human mind. Without an implicit affirmation of these principles no human thinking is possible. One of these basic principles is the affirmation of the existence of the "whereunto" of the dynamism of our intellect, that is, of the existence of God. Of course, many scientists, if told about this, would deny it. If and when they do, they are speaking no longer as scientists but as philosophers. They are no longer enjoying the competence which they may have in their respective fields. It is rather naive to believe that because a person is highly competent in physics, chemistry, physiology, psychology, and so on, he or she is also highly competent in philosophy!

Scientific work is highly technical and artificial. Within it there is no room for art, beauty, love, humor; there is no room in it either for God. When the scientist leaves the laboratory, he generally reassumes a more natural attitude. And then most of these values return in his life. This applies also to the "metaphysical soul" of knowledge. He may for instance, as a scientist, consider his little daughter as a very complex physiological system, as an infinitely complicated machine. But when he comes home, he considers her as a human being, as a person. And these are philosophical, not scientific, concepts.

Not only does he use philosophical terms in daily life but he also uses philosophical or metaphysical explanations. As Professor G. Isaye pointed out,[1] scientists in everyday situations continually admit such explanations which cannot be checked experimentally, neither directly nor indirectly. The scientific paper which he reads consists of a great number of letters arranged in a certain order. How does he explain this order? Like everybody else he attributes it to the intention of the author of the paper. How does he explain that the sounds emitted by a colleague in the laboratory make sense? It is because he considers him or her a conscious and intelligent being. Should he deny this, he too will reject this explanation in writing or in speech by arranging a certain number of signs in a certain order to convey his ideas.

Hence the scientist feels continually impelled to admit explanations which are not scientific but metaphysical. He does this, not as a scientist, but as a human person. Since life itself forces one to admit ideas and explanations that are metaphysical, why would he not consider the possibility of admitting the ultimate, all-embracing explanation of reality?

Some authors, such as Teilhard de Chardin, claim that they can arrive at God through science. He calls his *The Phenomenon of Man* a purely scientific memoir, and in it he arrives at the conclusion that the ultimate explanation of the universe lies in the Omega Point (God). In fact, Teilhard's work is not purely scientific. He uses a combination of philosophical and scientific data to arrive at his conclusion. His book centers around what he calls the law of complexity-consciousness: an increase in centro-complexity in matter is accompanied by a corresponding increase in consciousness.

How does he establish this essential law? It is done, not through scientific research, but through philosophical self-reflection.

Teilhard tried to widen the meaning and scope of science.[2] For him science studies all phenomena, whatever is given in human experience. Now some of these "givens" are known to us only through a process of philosophical reflection. Such is the phenomenon of self-awareness, of knowing that one knows, on which Teilhard insists so much in his work. Such a phenomenon is not a datum of scientific investigation in the generally accepted sense of this term. That is why so many scientists do not accept the "scientific" conclusions of Teilhard.

Teilhard's work is rather an example of a *philosophy of nature*, when that rather vague term is understood in the sense of an investigation in which the data of experience (everyday or scientific) are interpreted in function of metaphysical principles. Should the usual meaning of science be widened sufficiently to include such kind of study, Teilhard's essay would really be a scientific one. But the trend among scientists does not seem to be going in such a direction.[3]

The Essence Of God

WHILE I WAS TRYING to make a case in reason for the existence or the reality of God, I have already said a certain number of things about his essence or nature. It would be impossible for me to find out *whether* God is if I did not know at all *what* or *who* he is. That is why I started my investigation into God's existence by adopting a nominal definition of him. It contained two elements: infinity and necessity. The being whose existence I claim to have a right to affirm is one who is infinitely perfect and who exists necessarily.

Let us suppose, therefore, that my reader accepts this nominal definition of God and admits also that the first part of this work constitutes a vindication of my right of affirming the existence of such a being, thus to transform the nominal into a real definition. The problem then arises whether and how we might find out more about the nature or essence of this being.

Bergson has rightly asserted that "The nature of God will thus appear in the very reasons we have for believing in His existence."[1] The reason we have for believing, or rather for affirming, the existence of God is that we do so necessarily, although unthematically, in every affirmation and action through the dynamism of our intellect and of our will. There is in us a striving that goes beyond any limitation or finiteness toward the absolutely illimited, the intensively infinite. We know, or better we intend, God as the being who lacks all

119

limitation, who is infinite in every respect, who is infinitely perfect, who possesses every conceivable perfection to an infinite degree. We shall find out more about God by trying to study what these perfections imply when they are pushed to infinity.

Our knowledge of God differs from the knowledge we have of all other realities. That is why, before undertaking our exploration into the divine nature, it will be useful to say a few more words about the very peculiar way in which we know God.

How We Know God

The way in which we have established God's existence made it clear that we have no adequate concept of him. How would a finite mind, with finite concepts, provide an adequate concept for an infinite reality? We know God by striving for him with our intellect and our will, by pointing toward him with our spiritual faculties, by affirming and loving him. We know him only as the reality which lies beyond any reality of which we can have an adequate concept, as infinitely exceeding and transcending the ordinary objects of our knowledge.

Whenever we affirm something of God, we must correct our affirmation, since we are aware that it does not quite express what God really is. Whatever we say or think about God is partly false, and we are aware that it is partly false, yet we are forever unable to discover an affirmation which applies perfectly to him. Even the assertions which, philosophically speaking, describe God least inadequately contain such an element of falsity. Thus, when we say that God is the *whereunto* of our intellectual dynamism, we use a spatial image (whereunto) that does not quite express what we mean. When we call God Pure Act, Infinite Perfection, Being Itself, these terms evoke in our mind finite concepts of act, perfection or being, which we try to correct by adding to them the appropriate qualifier (pure, infinite, itself).

Of God we may say that he is being, intelligent and good. But we may also say that he is not being, not intelligent, not good. These denials are true insofar as they deny of God the only kind of being, intelligence and goodness of which we have an adequate concept: finite being, finite intelligence and finite goodness. In that sense we should rather say that God is superbeing, superintelligent, supergood: we keep the attributes affirmed of him, we deny their limitation and we entrust them, as it were, to our intellectual dynamism, so that the latter may transform them into something which we, with our finite minds, are unable to express.

In technical language we speak of analogy, of analogous concepts or terms. A concept is analogous when it applies to its objects partly in the same sense and partly in a different sense. It differs from univocal and equivocal terms or concepts. A term or concept is univocal when it applies to its objects in the same sense, as the concept of goat, oak or table when taken in the ordinary sense of these words. A term is equivocal when it applies to its objects in totally different, unrelated ways, as for 'ring', used for something around the finger, something on which boxers slug it out and that which comes to us from the telephone. An analogous term or concept combines equality and inequality: it is a synthesis of affirmation and negation, of like and unlike. God is good; my mother is good; wine is good. As applied to these three realities, the word 'good' keeps its basic meaning: all three of them are valuable, desirable, lovable, attractive, enriching. Yet the goodness of my mother and that of a glass of champagne are quite different, and even more different is the creaturely goodness of both of them from the uncreated, infinite goodness of God.

We have an idea of the difference between "mother" and "wine"; therefore we are also aware of the extent to and the meaning in which the term 'good' applies to either of them. We are also in some way aware of the difference between the two finite realities on the one hand and the infinite reality on the other hand. We are aware of this difference negatively: the former are finite; the latter is not. We are also aware of the difference positively: the former are objects of our knowledge; the latter is its whereunto, its horizon. It is undeniable, however, that we have a much vaguer idea of what 'good' means when we apply it to God than when we predicate it of creatures, but we are not totally at a loss.

Another way of explaining this state of affairs is to say that when speaking of God, we *mean* more than we can picture or represent; we *intend* more than we can express. This requires a few words of explanation. Whenever we know something, we always use both our intelligence and our senses. This is unavoidable because it results from our very nature: we are both spirit and body; we are embodied spirits. Now, our bodies are material, confined within the boundaries of space and time. That is why whatever we picture or represent in our mind is material, submitted to the same spatial and temporal limitations. This is true not only of our senses and imagination but also of our intelligence when we consider it in its relation to sense knowledge. This aspect of our intelligence was called *ratio* (reason) by Aquinas, and it is known in modern philosophy as the *understanding*. It corresponds to the *intelligence* of experimental psychology. But in the same way in which our spiritual soul, while animating our material body, also transcends it, so our mind, while always turned to the senses in its lower reaches, always transcends their domain in its higher reaches. The ancients called this aspect *intellectus*, and the moderns know it as *reason*. Because of our intellect or reason, our concepts and judgments, while rooted in space and time, are able to point beyond them. Thus, when we try to form an idea of our soul, we may have vaguely before our mind the picture of a very subtle fluid, which perfuses all our limbs. Yet, while using this material image, we know very well that our soul is not such a fluid; we intend or mean something different from the material fluid, be it ever so subtle that we represent or picture. Something similar happens when we affirm the existence of God. We picture or represent him always, more or less vaguely, as some kind of material, finite, spatiotemporal reality. But on account of the dynamism of our intellect and of our will we can intend and mean a reality which lies beyond all these limitations.

Thus we come back to and we may better understand what we said before about God being not the *what* but the *whereunto* of our knowledge. We are capable of representing in our mind that which we know (the *what*), whereas we can only mean the *whereunto* of our knowing and willing activity. Yet this "whereunto" is at least implicitly coknown and coaffirmed by us whenever we know any object at all. It has been shown above that it is only because our intellectual dynamism is always poised toward the infinite whereunto that we can have objects in our mind. Thus it is clear that analogical knowledge is not some kind of artificial way of knowing, which we use only when our ordinary knowledge lets us down. It is rather our primary way of knowing, since it is a condition of the possibility of all our human knowledge.

It is worth insisting upon this point, because some philosophers have the impression that knowledge through analogy is some kind of "gimmick" to which we have recourse when our real knowledge no longer will do. We would use the concepts which we derive from ordinary knowledge, blend them with negations and "sublimations" and in this way construct some artificial kind of knowledge serving as a crutch where our mind can no longer advance in its usual way. This impression gains strength when, as is generally done, our analogical knowledge of God is presented as a specific application of "analogical knowledge" in general.

This is far from being the case. Our analogical knowledge of God is, with its counterpart knowledge of "materiality," unique of its kind. It is not a species in a genus. It is not artificially knocked together with bits and pieces of so-called ordinary knowledge. It is as primordial as the latter. Whenever we get into existential contact with some everyday reality through knowledge, we form of this reality a universal univocal concept. But this knowledge possesses a double fringe of knowledge through analogy that remains mostly unthematic but is nevertheless so real that without it there would be no object in the mind.

Our concepts of everyday objects consist of a unified multiplicity. The multiplicity comes from the senses; the unity, from the intellect. Via the senses our intellect is in contact with the multiplicity of matter, and ultimately with the pure multiplicity of materiality, of what used to be called "prime matter." On the other hand, the unity which our intellect imposes on the multiplicity submitted by the senses refers, beyond the unity of "being as such" (*ens commune*), to the illimited unity of Being Itself (*Ipsum Esse Subsistens*). Both materiality and Being Itself are coknown and coaffirmed unthematically in every object whose existence we affirm. And this coknowledge is analogical. Our every affirmation always embraces the whole of reality, from pure potency to Pure Act. Our (univocal) explicit knowledge of everyday objects is accompanied and carried by an (analogical) implicit knowledge of materiality and of God. And it is only because of this fringe of analogical knowledge that we enjoy intellectual knowledge at all. Without it our knowledge would only be that of the highest of all animals; it would not be human knowledge.[2]

What is thus known analogically in our ordinary knowledge is not the object itself, say a child or a town; but of this child and this town we implicitly affirm that while they are rooted in materiality, they really ARE. We predicate BEING of them. And the limited being of these realities is projected against the horizon of illimited being. They become objects for our mind only because, through and beyond them, our intellect intends the infinite being.

We may have the impression that when we say that God *is*, we attribute being to him as we have come to know it in our everyday experience. Things are; God is. We know things; from them we find out what *being* is, and we attribute this being, duly amplified to infinity, to God. But this is a false impression, as well explained by Professor J. Defever:

> It is because we know implicitly what God is that we know what things are, and not the other way around. To be sure, the proper determinations of things come from the things themselves, through the sense experience we have of them. But that precisely these determinations are the determinations of the *being* of things, that these things are *intelligible* and *existing* according to the quiddity, this we would not be able to know if we did not know implicitly what God is, that he is unlimited being and intelligibility. In order for the quiddity to become intelligible in act, the intelligence must free it from matter; in order to free it from matter, the intelligence must assume it in its movement toward the ultimate end, which is the intelligibility and the existence of Being itself.[3]

All of this goes to show that our analogical knowledge of God is not some kind of artificial knowledge which we put together with bits and ends of ordinary knowledge. It is rather a component of all our ordinary knowledge, one of its two flanks, of which we are generally not aware, which remains prereflective, but without which our everyday knowledge would not be human knowledge.

It also goes to show that although we distinguish three steps in our analogical knowledge—God is a being (positive), God is not a being (negative), God is a Superbeing, Being Itself (supereminence)—we "live" these three steps together; none precedes the others. It is only when we reflect upon this datum of our innermost experience that we have to distinguish the steps and put a sequence among them.

What is true of the analogical affirmation of being is also true of the transcendental attributes of being, of the pure perfections, which, as they imply no limitation in their essential nature, are convertible with being.

Our analogical knowledge of God and of his attributes may be hazy, because it is lost in the infinite distance which separates it from its objects. It is by no means artificial. It is a condition of the possibility of all our human knowledge and activity.

By way of conclusion we might say that when we have the concept of some finite reality in our mind, we may call it a thought thought, in the sense that it is something which we think. This thought is the *content* of our thinking. But what or who is the *subject* of this thinking, what or who thinks this thought? It is the thinking thought in me; it is I myself, the pure subject, as thinking. Thought thoughts are always somehow connected with matter, with space and time. They cannot really represent the infinite being. But I, as thinking thought, am able to point, am always pointing, beyond all finite realities, toward their inexpressible archetype, and it is this unceasing referring of every content of my consciousness to its infinite horizon which makes the human person capable of knowing objects as objects, of designating and naming them, of speaking, of using real language, of developing a culture and a civilization. It is the absence of such an intellectual dynamism that explains why animals, although capable of communicating, are unable really to speak, to use an authentic language.

All of this explains why our knowledge of God is both ineradicable and very scanty and hazy. It explains why count- less uneducated people are absolutely certain that God exists yet are unable to answer the objections made against the reasons they may bring forward to justify their conviction. It explains why the way we *picture* God in our mind is always false. For we never see him directly but only, as it were, out of the corner of our mind's eye. When we turn our gaze upon him to see him more clearly, he disappears, for he is never an object, but that which lies beyond all objects, that which makes objects as such possible.

After having said a few words about our way of knowing God, I must now try to find out, to some extent, what God is. As mentioned above, this investigation has to be made in function of a philosophical system. And there will be no time to explain this system. We shall have to take it over ready-made, apply it to our topic and see whether its conclusions make sense. The system which I shall use in my attempt to investigate God's nature or essence is the traditional, or "perennial," philosophy which had its start with Aristotle (384-322 B.C.), peaked in St. Thomas Aquinas (1224-1274) and, after having been made more aware of its own transcendental component by Joseph Maréchal (1878-1944), has been presented with a new vitality by such authors as Karl Rahner, Emerich Coreth, Bernard Lonergan and others.

The picture of God's nature which I reach in this way makes real sense in most respects: in most, but not in all, respects. There are flaws, obscurities. In order to take care of them, I shall try to use, very tentatively, another tack. Would modern *process* philosophy not help us shed some light upon these darker spots? Although I am not sure that this approach is satisfactory, I present it for what it is worth. The reader will have to decide whether this is mere eclecticism or a valid attempt to think through along the lines of perennial philosophy.

6. God's Nature according to Traditional Philosophy

I SHALL FIRST EXAMINE what reason seems to tell us about God *in himself*. Next an attempt will be made to find out how it conceives God *in his relation to the world*.

I. GOD IN HIMSELF

Having briefly explained how we can know God, we must now try to find out more about what he is. We know him as infinitely perfect, as possessing all perfections without any restriction or limitation to an infinite degree. Thus we might get to know him better by considering some of the main perfections and trying to reach some idea, be it ever so hazy, of how they look when pushed into infinity.

Some perfections are essentially limited. Their very idea implies limitation, excludes infinity. They are known as *mixed* perfections: thus, to be healthy, handsome, clever, a good athlete, a great painter. All of these qualities or achievements suppose that their possessor has a body and is a material being living within space and time. Such perfections cannot be *formally* (in their exact sense) attributed to God. They may be *virtually* attributed to him, as to their ultimate cause, as to one who is capable of producing them in finite beings.

Other perfections do not imply limitation in their very definition. They are known as *pure* perfections. Such are unity, truth, goodness, intelligence, consciousness, will, freedom, love, activity, power. All of them may and should be attributed to God formally, in their exact sense, without any limitation or restriction.

I shall consider here only the first three—unity, truth and goodness—since they contain most of the others. But let me first give a few words about the basis of all these perfections, God's very being.

God is infinite being. He is not A being; he is *being itself*. A being implies limitation; therefore this title does not apply to God. The beings of our experience cannot be said to *be* being; they have or share it. There is in them another component which restricts their being and makes them be *what* they are. Their existence is limited by their essence, their "whatness." In this sense of the word 'essence' God has no essence, since his being is unlimited: he possesses, or rather he is, the fullness of existence without any limitation. However, the term 'essence' is also used to express "that which makes a being into that which it is." In that sense we may speak of a divine essence. That which makes God that which he is is *being*. God's essence is to be. In him essence and being, essence and existence, are identified.

A. The Unity of God

Traditional ontology demonstrates that all beings are one, that being and unity are convertible, that the more a being is, the more it is one. Since God is infinite being, he is also infinitely one. It follows that in God there·are neither parts nor components. If there were any parts in him, they would be, as such, in potency to union; they would require some extraneous cause to unify them. But there can be no potency in God, nor can any extraneous influence on him be admitted.

Hence in God there is no distinction of existence and essence, of substance and accidents, of faculties, properties or

attributes. In us intelligence, will, the faculties we possess, the
virtues we have developed, are accidents, that is, realities
which are not us, but which inhere or exist *in* us. We *have* them;
we cannot be said to *be* they. God, on the other hand, is pure
substance, existing in and by and for himself, without any
accidents, without any added modifications or qualifications.
We should not say that he has an intelligence and a will, that he
possesses goodness and justice. He IS all these things. He is
intelligence, will, love, goodness, power and justice. In the
divine simplicity all these perfections coincide, somewhat as
the different colors of the rainbow, when brought to their
highest possible intensity, merge into the one dazzling light of
the sun.

Therefore God's intellect is identical with his will; his
goodness is identical with his justice. When realized in finite
ways, goodness and justice are distinct perfections. When
carried to infinity, they coincide with all other perfections. Yet
their finite effects in creatures remain distinct, so that we have a
reason for speaking of them as distinct perfections in God. But
that reason lies not in God but in his creatures. God possesses
without any distinction perfections which, when realized in
creatures, are clearly distinct.

God has no accidents. Now among accidents one of the
most important is *relation*. In God, as known by reason, there
are no relations. God is related to nothing: he is relative with
respect to nothing; he is the Absolute. Yet we cannot help
thinking of God as related. Thus, when we say that God creates
the universe, we necessarily think of him as its creator, as
standing to it in the relation of a creator to his creature. When we
say that God knows and directs everything in the universe, we
think of him as having with respect to everything in the universe
a relation of knowledge and providence. Traditional philosophy
is well aware of this, but it calls these relations purely mental:
they exist only in our mind, not in God. We are really related to

God; he is not really related to us. The relation is one-sided, not reciprocal.

God is one also in the sense that there is only one God, that God is, of his very nature, unique. This follows from his infinity. If there were several Gods, they would differ in something: each one of them would have to possess something the others lacked or lack something the others possessed. Hence none of them would be infinitely perfect; none of them would really be God.

The divine unity implies also the divine immutability, the property of being absolutely unchangeable. Beings that change are not perfectly one, since they become what they were not and are no longer what they were. Moreover, should they change, something in them changes while something remains unchanged. Therefore God cannot change: he is immutable. This is evident also from the fact that God is pure perfection. Every change implies a change from potency to act, which is excluded from God. Changing would imply the acquisition of a new perfection or the loss of a former one, both of which are incompatible with God's infinite perfection. Here again we cannot escape the impression that when God creates, when he acts in the world, when, as christians believe, he becomes man, he changes. Traditional philosophy explains these apparent changes by insisting that in those cases the only thing which changes is the world, the thing on which God acts, the human nature assumed by God. This does not sound very convincing, and we shall return to it.

Connected with the divine immutability is God's eternity. Change and time go together. Where nothing changes there is no time. God is not in time; he is eternal. Eternity is the permanence in being that belongs to the infinite being, whereas time is the one which belongs to finite material beings. The traditional definition of eternity comes from Boethius (fifth to sixth century A.D.). He called it *interminabilis vitae tota simul et perfecta possessio*: the perfect possession of unending life all at once. We receive our existence, as it were, drop by drop, moment after moment. We never live more than the present instant of it. Suppose that these countless instants were to coalesce, so that we might live in one of them what is now stretched out along the course of time. And suppose that this one unbelievably rich moment would last forever. We would have some idea of what is meant by this "possession of life all at once." But even so we would still be far from God's eternity, since our life had a beginning and our possession of it is far from perfect. Eternity excludes any beginning, any ending and any change. It is coextensive with all times, which means that all times are present to it. For God there is no future, no past; everything is always present to him. We find it very difficult to understand or to imagine this. A simple example may help us to some small extent. When we watch a parade on street level, we can only see one group at a time. Should we watch it from a police helicopter, we might be able to see all the groups at once. Because we rose in space, our gaze becomes able to take in the whole parade. This may help us to get an inkling of how for God all space and all time may be eternally present.

B. The Intelligence of God

Traditional philosophy establishes that every being is true. Truth and being are convertible. This means that the more a being is, the more it is true. But what does "true" mean in this context? It is that every being is intelligent and intelligible, knowing and knowable, to the extent that it is. Since God infinitely is, he is infinitely intelligible and infinitely intelligent. He is the subsistent Intellection, the Supreme and Infinite Idea, the Infinite Spirit.

When I say that God is supremely intelligible, I mean that there is in him no darkness, no opacity, not a single irrational component. True, God is not fully intelligible for us: not, however, on account of any lack of intelligibility in him, but because of an excess of it. God is for the eye of our mind what the sun is for the eyes of our body. The sun is the most visible object in our experience. It is so visible that we cannot look at it; it dazzles and blinds our eyes. So does the infinite intelligibility of God overwhelm the eye of our mind. He is and will remain for us the incomprehensible, unfathomable mystery, not because of a lack but because of an excess of intelligibility.

God is also infinitely intelligent. First he knows himself wholly and always. He is perfectly identified with himself, perfectly self-present, without any unconsciousness. He is Self-Identity, Self-Consciousness. This is worth insisting upon, not only because some philosophical systems, influenced by psychoanalysis, claim that the Unconscious comes first in reality, as the creative matrix from which all consciousness slowly emerges, but especially because pantheism, in the strict sense of the word, teaches that the Absolute passes, if not chronologically, at least logically or ontologically, from unconsciousness to consciousness. Now this is quite true for our finite human mind.

We started life unconsciously, and our consciousness slowly emerged in its contact with reality. At first we were conscious only of other persons (generally first of our mother), then of other things and only later of our own selves. It may be safely asserted that we should never have reached the stage of self-awareness if we had not first become aware of other persons and things. Strict pantheists apply to God what is true of human beings. That is why one of the most typical features of this kind of pantheism is God's need of creation. They argue as follows: If God were alone, he would be unable to know the "other"; hence he would also be unaware of himself. Therefore he had to produce the "other" unconsciously, necessarily, somewhat as a tree produces branches, twigs and leaves. He would eventually become aware of this "other" (the Universe) and thus reach self-consciousness.

This conception of a God who passes from an initial stage of unconsciousness to self-consciousness is unacceptable. This is not the God for whose existence a case may be made in reason. An unconscious God is an imperfect, limited God, one beyond whom our mind strives, and therefore no God at all. The whereunto of our intellectual dynamism is a being who is perfectly self-luminous, self-present, infinite Self-Consciousness.

I shall later establish that the whole of reality derives from God and is forever creatively held in existence by him. It follows that since God is total self-awareness, he knows the whole of reality. Some of the problems connected with this kind of divine knowledge will briefly be considered later on.

C. The Will of God

The third attribute which traditional philosophy predicates of being is goodness. Being and goodness are convertible. To the extent that a reality is, it is good. Since God is infinite being, he is infinitely good: he is infinite goodness. In this context the term 'good' does not mean kind, helpful, charitable; it means "object of the will," lovable, desirable, aimed at.

In connection with God's creatures this means that all of them are drawn to him. This is the goodness which reason discovers in the Supreme Being. Aristotle emphasized it when he affirmed that the Unmoved Mover moves "by being loved": *"Kinei hôs erômenon."* When in this connection we say that God is good, we mean that all creatures love him, each one according to its degree of being.

Does God's goodness also imply that he loves creatures, that he cares for them, that he desires to make them as happy as possible? This is not so evident. Aristotle never mentioned anything of the kind. More surprising is that St. Thomas too does not attribute this kind of goodness to God in the article of his *Summa* which considers God's goodness. He does mention it to some extent in the question which treats the will of God. There he writes, "If natural things, in so far as they are perfect, communicate their good to others, much more does it pertain to the divine will to communicate by likeness its own good to others as much as possible. Thus, then, He wills both Himself to be and others things to be; but Himself as the end, and other things as ordained to that end, inasmuch as it befits the divine goodness that other things should be partakers therein."[1]

Thus we see that what traditional philosophy, in its most representative spokesman, has to tell us about God's love for his creatures is that "it pertain[s] to the divine will to communicate by likeness its own good to others as much as possible. Thus then, He wills . . . other things to be."

Moreover, we should keep two other points in mind. First, God is not related to creatures. There is no real relation of love from God to creatures. Second, even if we feel entitled to attribute to God all pure perfections to their highest degree, it is not certain that we may do so with what is known as perfect love, in the sense of a love by which one loves another as oneself. This is obviously a mixed, not a pure perfection. It is impossible for the Infinite Being to love any other being as he loves himself, since he is infinitely lovable and no other being is.

From all this it is evident that reason as such gropes in the dark about God's love for his creatures. We know that *God is love* not from philosophy, but from revelation.

D. The Personality Of God

Is God a person? The answer to this question depends on what is meant by a person. If we mean, with traditional philosophy, that a person is a spiritual substance, a being endowed with an intellect and a will, then God is the supreme person, since he is infinite spirit, since he is identically infinite intelligence and infinite will. If, however, we add to this that a person is an intersubjective being, an individual who is necessarily in relation with others of a kind, then God is not a person. For the reason there is only one God, there can be no others of his kind. Thus in the sense of "one amongst others," of "one over against others," God is not a person.

Thus it is good to think of God both as a person and as some impersonal reality: as a person, in order to be aware of him as conscious, knowing, loving; as some impersonal reality, in order to emphasize the fact that he has no equals, that he is all-encompassing, all-pervading.* These two seemingly incompatible ideas have somehow to be kept together in order for us to get some idea of the infinite mystery of God.

Reason left to its own devices does not know of the divine Trinity, of the three "persons" which the christian faith professes in God. Nevertheless some great philosophers, both medieval and modern, have speculated about this mystery. In the case of the former these speculations may have been more theological than philosophical. This is not the case, however, with such modern thinkers as Hegel, Blondel and Maréchal. Their example emboldens me to say a few words about the three divine persons.

Personality and intersubjectivity seem to go together. We find it difficult to conceive of a person who is all alone of his kind, without any equal with whom to commune. Yet such is the conception of God to which reason leads us. There is only one God. Although God has created human persons, he does not need them: he might have eternally existed without them. This eternal solitude of the infinite being puzzles us.

---

*God as God belongs to no gender: he is neither male nor female. If his revelation had occurred in a matriarchal society, he might have revealed himself as a Mother. Strictly speaking he is neither a father nor a mother: he infinitely transcends these finite categories.

Might it not be said, then, that our mind welcomes the revealed doctrine of the Trinity, of the three divine persons in the one divine nature? Reason is not only unable to discover it but is even unable to understand fully this doctrine. Yet it is not entirely unprepared for it. We know from reason that God is infinite self-consciousness and self-volition. He knows himself and he loves himself with a knowledge and a love that are identical with himself.

> If one likes to use the conceptual symbolism of Fichte, one may continue to say (by transposing the doctrine of the Trinity, which is revealed as an object of our faith, but which is also strongly suggested by the analogy of our reason) that the Absolute Principle (the Father) objectivates himself, that is, reflects himself in the Word, and that Love, which caused the Word (the Son) to be begotten by the Father, reduces the Word himself to the identity of the original principle. Love, or the Holy Spirit, is the reciprocal synthesis of the Father and the Son. Thus there is within God himself a perfect closed cycle, possessing three equal moments, sharing the same divine essence, but distinct by their relative opposition: Principle, Form, reciprocal Love; Position, Reflection, Synthesis.[2]

Our reason easily understands that there are these three "aspects" in God. But it does not understand how these aspects can be three different "persons," although the word 'person' should be understood here, not in the modern sense of a center of consciousness, an originating source of thinking and willing, but rather in the traditional sense of "subsistence." Even in the triune God there is only one I, one who knows and who loves. There is only one consciousness, shared in mutual relation of opposition by the three subsistences. It follows that those who speak of divine intersubjectivity, divine society, mutual giving, receiving and loving in the Trinity, incur the danger of tritheism. Part of the mystery of the trinitarian dogma consists precisely in that we find it impossible to conceive a position which avoids both errors of "modalism" (the three are only "modes" or "aspects" of the one God) and of tritheism (there are, in fact, three gods).

The following passages from Hegel and from Blondel show that some leading philosophers do not consider that human reason knows nothing about the Trinity. Hegel writes:

> To thinking reason God is not emptiness, but Spirit; and this characteristic of Spirit does not remain for it a word only, or a superficial characteristic; on the contrary the nature of Spirit unfolds itself for rational thought, inasmuch as it apprehends God as essentially the Triune God. Thus God is conceived as making Himself an object of Himself, and further the object remains in this distinction in identity with God: in it God loves Himself. Without this characteristic of Trinity, God would not be Spirit, and Spirit would be an empty word.[3]

> This is, in other words, the nature of God. When God is made a subject, this means that he begets his Son, the world. He realizes himself in this reality, that appears as other—yet he remains identical with himself . . . and in the other he merely unites himself with himself, and thus he becomes Spirit.[4]

Blondel, on the other hand, is aware that for the christian the Trinity is a mystery, lying essentially beyond the range of reason. He speaks of it more reservedly than Hegel:

> Metaphysics which can and must justify the mysterious aseity of the necessary Being is not without any reasonable argument to catch a glimpse of the fact that God is good, in a way which, to be sure, is ineffable for us, but which nevertheless allows us to suspect, if we are bold enough to use human words, the intimate generosity, the sublime self-devotion, the loving exchange that constitutes the blessed eternity of the One whom Aristotle had already been able to call the pure Act and the Thought of Thought, without reaching the full idea of charity, without which the framework leaves unoccupied the place that is ready for the vivifying Spirit.[5]

And again,

But once philosophy normally reaches the mysterious notion of aseity, should we not discover in it a meaning which does not let this notion fall back into the night of a word devoid of content? And as we start from the first *Cause* and call it *Ratio sui*, does this very expression not imply that an intimate and fertile life brings about in it an eternal generation? And does this notion itself not necessarily suggest something that is analogous to what happens in man's innermost life and heart, paternity, filiation and love?[6]

II. GOD'S RELATION TO THE WORLD

A. Creation[7]

The former ways of "demonstrating" God's existence had no trouble showing that the universe with all it contains has been caused by God, since they reached God as the First Cause. If the unmoved mover of Aquinas' First Way is considered not only as it was by Aristotle, as the final cause of everything, but as the efficient cause of all beings, it follows that every finite reality derives from God.

It has been shown above that the two main objections generally made to this approach can be answered. They were (1) that it took for granted the principle of metaphysical causality, to which serious objections had been made both by Hume and by Kant, and (2) that it passes from finite effects to an infinite cause. For those who are satisfied with the way in which these objections have been answered, the First Way of St. Thomas holds good, and it is evident that God is the supreme cause of the whole universe.

What I have tried to establish in my "vindication" is that the objects of our experience are "intelligible" only if we refer them to the infinite reality. I arrived at God not as the cause of everything but as the one I coknow and coaffirm every time I get to know some reality. I have shown that everything derives its intelligibility from God. Does it follow that everything also derives its existence from him?

For anybody who admits with traditional philosophy that truth and intelligibility are convertible with being, it does so follow. To be true, to be intelligible, in the full ontological sense of these words, is the same as to be. That which causes things to be true and intelligible causes them also to be. Hence, since all realities derive their intelligibility from God, they likewise derive from him their existence, their reality, their being.

In other words—and this no longer supposes that one admits traditional ontology—the metaphysical principle of efficient causality is contained within and follows from the principle of intelligibility. It does not seem possible to answer Kant's objections without showing that the principle of metaphysical causality, as implied in the principle of intelligibility, is implicitly affirmed by us in our every affirmation. That is what I have tried to do.

Every reality derives its being wholly from God. Thus the divine causality differs from all the ones we know in our experience. When human persons cause something to exist (a chair, a poem, a child), they cause the "whatness," not the "thatness," of their effect. They transform something preexisting (wood, words, proteins) into something else. This is not the case with God. Since absolutely everything depends totally on him, he cannot use any preexisting materials when he causes something to exist. Finite causes produce something out of something; the infinite first cause produces everything out of nothing. This is not in the sense that "nothing" is the material out of which everything is produced, but in the sense that there simply is no preexisting material. To produce out of nothing is traditionally called "to create." God creates everything that exists outside of himself. He not only makes them *what* they are; he also explains *that* they are. He not only makes them; he makes them be.

The idea of creation was unknown to the great philosophers of antiquity. Both Plato and Aristotle admitted the preexistence of some component of reality (matter, chaos, receptacle) which did not derive from God and out of which or in which the universe originated under the influence of God. This idea is unacceptable. A God who depends in any way whatsoever on anything preexisting is known right away as one than whom somebody more perfect may be conceived, as a limited God. Our intellectual dynamism strives beyond this "god" for an infinitely perfect God.

But why should we not say that God made the universe out of himself, out of his own divine substance? Why could it not be produced by him in the way branches and leaves are produced by a tree? This doctrine has been proposed by some great philosophers, especially by Plotinus (third century A.D.) and by the neo-Platonists. They called this way of causing the universe "emanation."

In a certain sense creation is emanation. Aquinas called it "the emanation of the whole of being from the universal cause" (*Summa Theologica*, I, q. 45, a.1). In another sense, however, it is not. Emanation is generally construed as a blind, unconscious, necessary "flowing out" of all things from their source. In that sense it implies an imperfection, a limitation in God, since in this hypothesis God *must* create: he is not free in doing so. Moreover, the theory of emanation leads easily into pantheism, to the doctrine which claims that there is only one substance, one reality, of which everything else is a part, an aspect, a mode.

Since God did not make creatures out of some preexisting material or out of his own substance through emanation, it follows that he made them out of nothing.

God is the efficient cause of the universe. But this can easily be misunderstood and threaten the divine transcendence. When we consider God as the maker of the universe, we may be tempted to introduce him, as its first all-important link, into the chain of causes and effects which constitute the universe, thus to make him a part of it and rob him of his transcendence. We may avoid this by remembering that God is the universal cause not of the becoming but of the *being* of the universe. Chains of causes and effects are found only when we have to do with causes of becoming. We tend to forget that God not only causes all things but he causes them *to be*.

Thinking of God as the efficient cause of the universe may also endanger his immanence, make the distinction between him and his creatures too strong and thus set up two realities whose combination it is very difficult not to consider greater than each one of them. This danger might be avoided by thinking of God producing the universe, not in the way in which a carpenter produces a chair, but rather in the way in which we produce our ideas. We are not merely their efficient cause; we are also to some extent their exemplary and their quasi-formal cause, their animating principle. However, when we conceive of God's creative activity in this way, another danger occurs: that of pantheism. God's "relation" to his creatures is unique. To understand it we must combine different types of causality— efficient, exemplary and quasi-formal—and correct each one by means of the others, because none of them will do in isolation. The following considerations may help us keep this in mind.

1. Creation is not an event. It never happened, in the strict sense of the word. Events happen in space and time. But space and time exist only in the universe and with it. Strictly speaking, the universe never started to exist, in the sense at least that there never was a time when there was no universe, since time and the universe come and go together. God did not create the universe in time and in space; the universe, space and time were all created together.

It is quite true that we cannot imagine the absence of time, since the time we imagine is the a priori form of our imagination. We can imagine things only in it. This does not mean that there exists no objective time, one which is more than a form of our inner senses. However, the universe does not exist in this real time, but it exists in the universe. We do not perceive real time as it is in itself; we can get an idea of it only by using our imaginary time, the a priori form of our inner senses, in which we imagine whatever we imagine.

2. Not only did God never really "start" creating but he also never "stops" creating. Causes of becoming may start and stop their activity, but not the universal cause of being. As long as some reality exists, God causes it to exist and in that sense creates it. We too easily imagine that we depend on God somewhat in the way in which a table depends on the carpenter who made it. When the carpenter stopped making the table, the latter did not stop existing. Should God stop causing us to be, we would no longer exist. We should therefore rather imagine our dependence on God after the way in which a beam of sunlight depends on the sun or our ideas on the mind which thinks them. This continued creation is called *conservation*. God continually conserves every reality in being.

3. There is another way in which it is true to say that God never stops creating. In the preceding paragraph God was shown keeping in existence whatever exists. We have good reasons for admitting that he also continually causes to exist new realities which did not exist previously. Here, however, the term 'creating' is no longer taken in its full sense of an absolute beginning, of "making out of nothing," but rather in the sense of "causing some reality to transcend its own powers," thus to enable it to produce effects of which it would be incapable by itself.

As Teilhard de Chardin explained,[8] we have hitherto tried to explain whatever exists by means of two ideas: creation and transformation. Creation would explain the first origin of everything; it occurred only at the beginning. This initially created reality has ever since undergone transformations; it has been modified, rearranged, but nothing totally new has ever been added to it.

It does not seem possible to explain the real universe in this way. A new idea is required, that of *creative transformation*. It is not simply creation, because the new reality does not, strictly speaking, derive from nothing. Nor is it merely transformation, because the process results in something totally new, in a real increase in *being*. In this creative transformation, as explained by K. Rahner,[9] God inserts, as it were, his own divine causality into some finite causality and enables it to transcend its own potentialities, to produce effects which it is unable to produce if left to its own devices. This implies that creation, in this wider sense, is an ongoing process not only in the sense of conservation but also in the sense of a real expansion of being. God causes more realities to share his being; the universe continues to grow, to expand, not only spatially but also ontically. It does not seem possible to give a total explanation of the undeniable fact of cosmic, organic and human evolution without the help of this idea of "creative transformation."

4. It follows that the theory of universal evolution by no means contradicts the idea of universal creation. God creates through evolution. His creation was not ready-made from the first moment. That is why it might be useful to add to the imagery which many of us have derived from the Bible (God as the "maker" of heaven and earth) the image suggested by Aristotle and by Teilhard de Chardin: God as a center of powerful attraction, which first drew the universe out of nothingness, then continues to attract it to himself, unifying, complexifying it, enriching it with consciousness and self-awareness. This attraction is irresistible on the mineral and organic and sense level, where it explains the *upward* "grop-

ing" of evolution. On the human level this attraction is affected by human freedom, and it may be partially thwarted by it. It leads the universe in the direction of more being; in that sense it is an ongoing creation, but a creation through evolution, a creation in which the creatures themselves are actively engaged, so far as God enables them to transcend their own powers.

B. Does God Create Necessarily or Freely?

Whichever way we answer this question we run into difficulties. We are tempted to say that God must, of course, create freely. Freedom is a pure perfection which God possesses formally; not only does he possess it but, as explained above, he is *pure* freedom. How could we ever admit any kind of compulsion in the infinitely perfect being, whether this compulsion should come from without or from within? A God who is not free would be known to us as a finite God beyond whom the dynamism of our intellect keeps striving.

On the other hand, we have seen above that God is perfectly one, that although we cannot help making distinctions when we think or speak of him, there are no real distinctions in him. This implies that God *is* his creative activity. Since God is the absolutely necessary being, it seems to follow that his creative activity too is absolutely necessary.

The antinomy, however, is more apparent than real. We must keep in mind that the word 'necessary' is ambiguous. It may mean unfree, coerced, imposed from without or from within. In this sense we naturally consider it an imperfection. It may also mean not contingent, unable not to be. In this sense it looks to us like an ontological perfection. Thus when we wonder whether God exists necessarily or wills and loves himself necessarily, the best answer seems to be: he exists, he loves and wills himself both freely and necessarily. He cannot

not exist, not love and will himself, yet there is in this existence, this love and this volition not the slightest compulsion or coercion; this existence, love and self-volition are totally and freely welcomed by God.

Might we not say the same about God's creative activity: that it is necessary like God's own nature, love and volition, yet totally lacking in any kind of compulsion? This would become understandable if we say that God creates out of love. Something that is motivated by love is, insofar as it is thus motivated, free. That which is motivated by infinite love will necessarily happen, yet it will happen in total freedom.

This "necessity" of freely creating is not quite the same as the one which is to be admitted in God's existing, in his loving and willing himself. Without the latter God would not be himself, whereas this being himself is presupposed by any sharing of himself in creation.[10] Nor should we, if we admit that God's infinite goodness will necessarily induce him to share his being through creation, have to admit also that he will create the "best possible universe." The idea of a "best possible universe" might well be contradictory. Would a best possible universe not be an infinitely perfect universe? Such a one would coincide with God! If a universe is to be at all, it will necessarily be a finitely perfect one, hence one which is infinitely remote from God's own infinite perfection. A so-called "best possible universe" would be as remote from it as any other. It seems, therefore, that we may conclude: It makes sense to say that God, out of the superabundance of his love, will necessarily create some universe, but not necessarily this or that universe. It makes no sense to claim that he will necessarily create the "best possible universe."

What is God's purpose in creating? It cannot be anything finite or created, since God cannot be in need of anything of the kind. Therefore his purpose cannot be any other than God himself: not in the sense of the pantheists, for whom God needs creation to become truly himself, but in the line of what was said above of God's overflowing love, which wishes to share. God's purpose in creation may therefore be stated as follows: It is God's being, as to be shared by his creatures.

C. Divine Concurrence

If we admit that God creates all things and goes on continually creating them, we must also admit that he creates all their powers and activities. Since nothing outside of God is self-explaining, this applies also to every created activity. Translated into concrete language, this means: God actually causes chemicals to react together, trees to grow leaves and fruit, animals to run and to beget their young, human beings to see and hear, to think, to love and to make free decisions. This creative influence of God upon all activities and operations is traditionally known as *divine concurrence*.

Let us first consider it in activities that are determined, not free. Primitive man tended to attribute many finite activities directly to the Creator, and so did the Bible, and so continue to do many unsophisticated people. God flings the lightning, makes the sun shine, the rain and the snow fall. He sends drought, floods, epidemics, famine, health, fertility.[11] We are better aware at present that God does not directly cause these finite activities; he uses secondary causes. Science has made enormous strides in discovering these immediate causes or antecedents. To make of God the first link in a chain of such activities would render him finite and rob him of his transcendence. We should rather say that he creatively keeps in being finite realities which produce and insofar as they produce such effects. In this way we reject the idea of a "stopgap" God, one who is supposed to explain that which science cannot or cannot yet explain. For the last few centuries such a God has steadily been retreating before the progress of science.

It remains true that God is their transcendent, not their categorial, cause.[12] This does not mean that God uses finite causes as simple tools; it means rather that he animates them somewhat[13] in the way in which each one of us animates his or her own body. When I wish to say something, I contract many muscles in my throat and mouth. These muscular contractions may physiologically be totally explained by nervous impulses and patterns in the brain. Nowhere in this sequence would anybody be able to pinpoint where my human will, my desire to say something, intervenes. This whole physiological chain seems to run off without any voluntary intervention. Yet it is somehow caused, assumed, vivified, animated by my wish to say something. Anyone who denies this will animate his own chain of physiological antecedents and consequents in order to express a dissenting opinion.

In a somewhat similar way on the phenomenal level, in sense experience, where science operates, all natural actions and reactions seem to follow each other without any intervention of a higher causality. Yet they are all creatively carried and directed by the Supreme Cause.[14]

We should keep this way of conceiving divine concurrence in mind when we shall soon meet one of the most ticklish problems of natural theology. If God is the creative cause of man's free activities, how can we still say that man is free? We must try to understand that man's free activities are really his own while being kept creatively in existence by God. God creates human beings while and insofar as they are actually making a free decision, performing a free activity. Indirectly God creates this free activity. Thus in a novel or in a play, as pointed out by Professor J. F. Ross, the novelist or the playwright creates characters that freely operate on their own, although they are totally the products of the author's mind.[15]

Another point to keep in mind in order to understand how divine concurrence operates is the following. The higher, the more perfect a being is, the greater is the divine influx into its existence and its operations. On the other hand, the higher a being stands in the scale of beings, the more spontaneous its activities become, the more autonomy it possesses. In God's most perfect creature, the human person, this spontaneity and autonomy become freedom of choice, which looks somewhat like a sharing of God's own creative power. We notice, therefore, that while in the field of human relations the more a person depends on another person, the less autonomy and freedom the former possesses, in our relation with God the opposite is true: the more a creature depends on God, the more that creature becomes independent.[16]

D. Providence

God, as the universal intelligent cause of the universe, directs all his creatures, according to his purpose, toward their end. This activity by which God directs all created things is called providence. Now it is argued that in order to reach his purpose, God must be able to foresee what every one of his creatures will do in all possible circumstances. If he is unable to do this, it is difficult to see how he will infallibly reach the end which he intends. There is no difficulty in regard to creatures that are not endowed with freedom. Their activities are determined and may be foreseen with total accuracy by an omniscient mind. But how can God infallibly foresee the free activities of human persons? If God knows now what I shall do ten years from now, how can I still be said to be a free agent? Try as I may, I shall inevitably decide and act in the way foreseen by God. All my activities are predestined.

The problem of predestination has exercised the human mind for many centuries, especially as it applies to man's ultimate destiny. Shall I finish my life on earth in peace with God or in conflict with him? If God infallibly foresees the outcome, it is useless for me to exert any effort one way or the other. Fatalism seems to be the only reasonable attitude.

A first answer to the difficulty consists in pointing out that God does not *foresee* the future; he *sees* it. He is not in time; all times are forever present to him. He knows in his eternal now whatever I did, do or shall do in time. This answer, however, does not remove the difficulty. The question still remains how God knows my future free acts. Does he know what I shall do because I shall be doing it? In that case he derives some knowledge from me; he receives information "from without." This seems to be impossible, since God is omniscient and immutable, since he cannot be influenced by others. But if God does not know what I shall do because I shall do it, it looks as if I shall do it because he knows it. In that case, how can I still be said to be a free agent?

In the sixteenth century, when this problem was the focus of long and passionate discussions, two famous, conflicting theories were presented which deserve to be mentioned briefly. The first one was defended by Domingo Bañez, O.P. (1528-1604). Bañez introduced the hypothesis of a physical predetermination of the human will by God. He held that when a person is about to make a free decision, he is unable to do so without a last decisive impulsion deriving from God. This impulsion is not simply an invitation, an appeal (moral determination), but a *physical* influx upon the human will. Without it the free decision is not possible; with it it necessarily follows. Bañez undeniably safeguards divine omniscience. But, although he insists that God irresistibly impels the human person freely to perform his free action, it is very difficult to see how this action can really be free.

The other system is that of Luis de Molina, S.J. (1535-1600). He distinguished in God three kinds of knowledge: (1) the knowledge of vision, whereby God knows all that which actually exists; (2) the knowledge of simple intelligence, through which he knows everything which is possible; (3) a knowledge which stands between the two first ones, an intermediate knowledge (*scientia media*), which allows God to know what would occur (even freely, as the result of a free human decision) if something, which will never occur, should occur. If the South had won the Civil War, the history of the United States would have been quite different. Many events would have happened which, in fact, have never happened. Within this never-existing historical context many free decisions would have been made, which, in reality, have never been made. Molina claimed that through his "scientia media" God knows these events, these "futuribles," as they have been called.

This short introduction allows us now to explain Molina's clever system. God, in his omniscience, knows of an infinite number of ways in which the history of the universe might unfold. Among these infinite combinations there is one wherein every event (whether determined or free) would occur exactly in the way in which God wants it to occur, so that all of them together would lead to the final purpose which he has in mind. It is this world order which he sovereignly decides to create. In it all free creatures will freely perform the activities which bring about God's purpose in history. God knows all of them without deriving this knowledge from his creatures. Yet the free creatures remain free. In this way Molina hoped to have safeguarded both divine omniscience and human freedom.

The difficulty with this system is that the *scientia media* seems to imply a contradiction, since it implies the certain knowledge of something which is, of its very nature, uncertain, undetermined. It is very hard to see how that which remains forever "either-or" can ever infallibly be known as "precisely this."

These discussions no longer fascinate us the way they used to fascinate some of our forebears. We have become more modest, too; we do not believe that we can understand everything in the infinite mystery. We get the impression that there is a considerable amount of anthropomorphism in these speculations.

Moreover, we are more aware that God does not operate categorially in the universe. He does not compete with human beings.[17] Human free decisions do not conflict with God's influence on history. When a human person makes a free decision (the most autonomous activity in the universe), God creatively keeps in existence not only this human person in the very act of freely choosing but the free action itself. These considerations do not solve the problem, but they may make it less ominous.

God is infinitely mysterious. Human freedom is very mysterious. It is no wonder if their combination makes for one of the most mysterious problems of human existence.

E. The Problem of Evil

The philosophy of God is sometimes called *theodicy*, which means "a vindication of God." This refers to the most difficult part of the philosophical doctrine of God, as it treats the way of reconciling the existence of an infinitely powerful and infinitely good God with the countless evils that beset mankind. The problem has often been presented succinctly as follows: If God is almighty, he can prevent evil. If he is infinitely good, he wishes to prevent it. Yet evils occur. It follows that God either is not almighty or is not infinitely good, that God therefore is not God. The existence of evil demonstrates the nonexistence of God. This is a very serious objection, and we might as well admit from the start that although philosophy tries hard to offer some kind of answer to it, this answer is far from satisfying the mind.

The answer of traditional philosophy insists upon the fact that God never directly causes any evil. This would be difficult to admit if evil were a being, since all beings derive from God. But evil is said to be not a being, but the absence of a being that should be present: in technical language, a *privation*. Trees have no eyes and men have no wings. This is not an evil; it is an absence, not a privation, of some good. But when a robin has no wings or a man no eyes, we have a privation: we meet a case of evil.

Shall we say then that pain and sin are mere privations? Not even traditional philosophy defended this view. Pain is the repercussion upon sensibility or consciousness of some privation. The cells are not multiplying the way they should (a privation), and the cancer patient endures heavy pain. The will of the sadistic murderer is not intending its real end, moral goodness (a privation); he tortures his victim to death. His criminal act is not a mere privation, but the positive act of a deviating will.

There are two main kinds of evil: physical evil and moral evil. The former affects nature; the latter affects a person as person in one's free will. *Physical* evil refers to pain and suffering; *moral* evil, to what philosophers call immoral actions and theologians call sins. There is moral evil whenever a person's free will deviates from its right direction, refuses to heed the call of moral obligation or of duty. In this sense it is a privation: it lacks a goodness which it should have.

God does not directly intend or cause evil. But he intends or causes things from some of which some evil follows necessarily, from others of which some evil may follow. In the former case God is said to will that evil indirectly; in the latter he does not will it at all: he is said to tolerate it, to allow it to happen. Both the indirect willing (of physical evil) and the tolerating (of moral evil) can be explained by the fact that they happen in behalf of a greater good.

In the case of moral evil this greater good is human freedom. God tolerates moral evil as something which follows (not necessarily) from the greatest good conferred on his highest creature: man and his free will. If man is to be made capable of freely directing his own moral life, he will also be capable of performing immoral actions. God might have suppressed all possibility of moral evil by making a person a being determined in all actions, as are all other material creatures. But then a human being would no longer be a human being. Thus God is not the cause of moral evil, but he is the cause of the possibility of moral evil, a possibility which he accepted in view of the greatest created good: human freedom.[18]

This explanation of moral evil satisfies many minds. Not all, however. There are philosophers who wonder whether God might not have made all human beings so good that they would have freely abstained from all moral evil. Since he made some persons that way, it is difficult to see why he could not have made all of them in this way. It would lead me too far afield to discuss this question here. The reader may find such a discussion in the remarkable work of John Hick *Evil and the God of Love*, chapter fourteen.[19] Let me simply transcribe his conclusion:

> God can without contradiction be conceived to have so constituted men that they could be guaranteed always freely to act rightly in relation to one another. But He cannot without contradiction be conceived to have so constituted men that they could be guaranteed freely to respond to Himself in authentic faith and love and worship. The contradiction involved here would be a contradiction between the idea of A loving and devoting him/herself to B, and of B valuing this love as a genuine and free response to himself whilst knowing that he has so constructed or manipulated A's mind as to produce it. The imagined hypnosis case reveals this contradiction as regards the relation between two human beings and by analogy we apply the same logic of personal attitudes to the relation between God and man.[20]

In the case of physical evil the greater good on account of which God wills it indirectly is the orderly running of the universe. God wills the material universe as a whole at the service of the spiritual creature that is man. This universe is a very complex totality of countless mutually interacting elements. Sometimes two causal series which are unfolding normally their effects will cross each other with unexpected harmful effects for some creatures. Thus a geological causal series may bring about an earthquake at a certain spot. A biological series had produced on that same spot a beautiful stand of stately Douglas firs. The landslide resulting from the earthquake uproots and kills the trees. This is an instance of physical evil, one which most people accept without difficulty. They see that if there is to be a universe running according to its own laws, such events are bound to occur, and very few expect God to interfere continually to prevent them.

But suppose that instead of a stand of firs a large village, product of a long series of cultural events, occupies that spot. The earthquake and the landslide utterly destroys it; families are decimated, children are orphaned, epidemics rage unchecked, to bring in their wake many more deaths, untold suffering. This is the case of physical evil caused in exactly the same way as the previous one, but it will fill quite a number of people with serious misgivings about the goodness or the existence of God. Here the evil affects human beings; here the "privation" results in acute human suffering and pain.

Does God will these physical evils? He does, not directly, but indirectly. What he wills directly is the universe as a whole with its laws. But the unimpeded working of these laws brings about many instances of pain and suffering among animals and human beings. God wills this physical evil indirectly by willing the universe as a whole. In every ordered totality the more universal good has precedence over the less universal; individual members may have to be sacrificed for the good of the whole. Amputation of diseased limbs and the death of soldiers defending their country are two examples of this law.

The greater good on account of which God would here indirectly will physical evil is the unimpeded working of the laws of the universe. I am afraid that many readers will not accept this explanation. Might God not have ordained other laws of the universe, laws that would have led up to no such physical evil or, at least, to much less of it? Or might he not omnipotently intervene whenever the ordinary running of the universe results in too much suffering for men? It is difficult to give a negative answer to these questions. One who does is Teilhard de Chardin, and it might be worth our while to listen to what he has to say before we continue our discussion. Speaking of the difficulties which some people may meet against their religious faith, he says this:

> To my mind, this penumbra of faith is simply a particular case of the problem of evil. And I can see only one way of overcoming this *fatal* stumbling block. This is to recognize that if God allows us to suffer, to sin, to doubt, it is because he *cannot* here and now cure us and show himself to us. And, if he cannot do so, it is exclusively because we are still *incapable*, by reason of the present phase of the universe, of a higher degree of organization and illumination.
>
> Evil is inevitable in the course of a creation which develops within time. Here again the solution, which brings us freedom, is given us by evolution.[21]

Teilhard believes that in a static, nonevolving universe, created ready-made by God, it would be difficult to explain the presence of so much physical evil. This is not so, however, for an evolving universe.

> In the ancient cosmos, which was supposed to have come full-fledged from the hands of the Creator, it is obviously difficult to reconcile a world which is partially evil with the existence of a God who is both good and omnipotent. On the other hand, in our modern perspectives of a universe in the stage of *cosmogenesis* . . . how can we explain that so many good minds stubbornly refuse to see that, intellectually speaking, the famous problem has vanished? . . . The unavoidable counterpart of any success obtained in this way is that it has to be paid for by a certain proportion of waste products. . . . I repeat that there is nothing in this ontological (or better ontogenetical)

condition which impairs the dignity or limits the omnipotence of the Creator . . . . In itself mere unorganized multiplicity is not bad, but because it is multiple—that is, essentially subject to the influence of change in its arrangements—it can in no way advance toward unity without giving here or there rise to evil, through *statistical* necessity . . . . If (as we must, I believe, necessarily admit) there is for our understanding only one possible way in which God can create—that is, through evolution, by way of unification—evil is an unavoidable by-product; it looks like a shadow which cannot be separated from creation.[22]

We are told by Teilhard that God can create only through evolution and that an evolving universe necessarily involves, as by-products or waste products, evils of all kind. Does this not contradict God's omnipotence, which is, of course, implied by his infinite perfection? Not necessarily. Omnipotence requires that God be able to do, not absolutely everything, but only everything that is possible, not contradictory. Thus God cannot create female brothers or square circles; he cannot hate himself or do away with himself. All these things are contradictory. Teilhard seems to hold that creation without evolution and evolution without the by-products of evils are impossible or contradictory. He does not demonstrate this impossibility, and one might well doubt whether it is so evident. His optimism about having finally solved the problem of evil is rather premature. And we have to look elsewhere for a better justification of the presence of evil in God's creation.

F. Pain and Suffering as a Condition of Moral Growth

If it is difficult to admit with Teilhard that God cannot prevent the many evils that beset human beings, the only way of justifying their presence seems to consist in affirming that God allows them for some reason in order to obtain a greater good. Moral growth, the highest created good, requires a great amount of effort; it also requires a certain amount of pain and suffering. Soft living and moral living rarely go together. In this connection it might be worth our while to read a few passages which Maurice Blondel has devoted to pain and suffering. They may be found in his masterpiece *L'Action* (1893), which is a philosophical study, not a work on theology. Since Blondel is so little known in this country and since most of his writings have not been translated, I might be excused for quoting him at some length. Despite the rather old-fashioned nineteenth-century French style which he uses, his message remains very important.

> Since there is at the origin of the good action a principle of abnegation, of passion and of death, we must not be surprised if, in the expansion of the life of morality, we constantly meet with suffering and sacrifice . . . . It turns us away from willing the less and inclines us to will the more . . . . Man's heart is measured by the way he welcomes suffering, because suffering is in him the stamp of another than himself . . . . It is always different from what we expected, and under its blows even he who faces and desires and loves it cannot help hating it at the same time: it kills something in us to substitute something which is not from us. That is why it reveals to us this shocking lesson of our freedom and of our reason: we are not what we will; and in order to will all that which we are, which we ought to be, we must understand and accept its lesson and its benefaction.
>
> Thus suffering is in us like a sowing: through it something enters into us, without us, in spite of us; let us then receive it, even before knowing what it is. The farmer throws away his most precious grain; he hides it in the ground; he scatters it so that nothing of it seems to be left. But it is precisely because the seed is scattered that it can no longer be stolen; it rots in order to be fertile. Like this decomposition, pain is required for the birth of a fuller work. He who has not suffered from a thing neither knows nor loves it. And this teaching may be summarized in one word, but one needs a heart to grasp it: the meaning of pain is to reveal to us that which eludes knowledge and a selfish will; it is

the way of effective love, because it detaches us from ourselves to give the other one to us and to invite us to give ourselves to the other one.

It does not produce its happy effect in us without an active cooperation: it is a trial because it forces the secret dispositions of the will to manifest themselves. It spoils, embitters, hardens those whom it does not mellow and improve. As it upsets the balance of an indifferent life, it summons us to choose between the personal sentiment which impels us to withdraw into ourselves while violently excluding every intrusion, and the kindness which opens up to fecundating sadness and to the germs carried by the mighty waters of tribulation.

But suffering is not only a trial; it is a proof of love and a renewal of interior life, like a rejuvenating bath for action. It prevents us from getting used to this world, and leaves us in it as incurably uncomfortable . . . . It will always be new to say: wherever we turn, we are ill at ease. And it is good to feel it; the worst would be no longer to suffer, as if the equilibrium had been found and the problem already solved . . . . Suffering is the new, the unexplained, the unknown, the infinite, that runs through life like a revealing sword.

That is why we discover some kind of reciprocity or, so to speak, of identity between real love and active suffering. For without the education of pain one does not learn disinterested and courageous action. Love produces the same effects in the soul as death in the body: it transfers the one who loves into what he loves, and that which is loved into that which is loving. Therefore to love means to love suffering, because it means to love the joy and the action of the other one in us: a pain in itself lovable and beloved to which consent those who feel it and which they would not barter for all the sweetness of the universe. . . .

But there is more. Suffering is not only the trial and the proof of a generous and valiant will, it is also the effect and as it were the very act of love. For if it is true that we are more where we love than where we are, wherever our own will is covered and supplanted by a contrary will, it looks as if every action of personal interest is no longer a gain but a loss and as if every

seeming enrichment becomes a real impoverishment . . . .
Suffering is the path that marches and rises; and in order to
progress much, it is enough that we consent to be carried.
Happiness is not that which we have; it is that which we do
without, that of which we deprive ourselves. Thus even in the
good we do we must do it as not coming from us. Everywhere
the sacrifice of his own will is for man the road to life. That by
means of which we deprive ourselves is worth infinitely more
than that of which we deprive ourselves . . . .

Mortification is the real metaphysical experimentation
carried out on being itself. That which dies is that which
prevents us from seeing, from acting, from living. That which
survives is already that which is born anew . . . . Nobody
loves God without suffering; nobody sees God without dying.
Nothing reaches him that has not risen from death: no will is
good if it has not moved out of itself, wholly to make room for
the total invasion of his will.[23]

I do not claim that these explanations totally take care of
the problem of physical evil, of pain and suffering. They do not
remove the shock we feel in the presence of catastrophic or of
crushing suffering (the Holocaust) or of pain so extreme that the
sound moral reaction of which Blondel speaks seems to become
impossible. They do not explain the suffering of small children
afflicted before the awakening of their moral life. They do not
explain the suffering of animals. They take away some of the
sting; they do not remove it entirely.

G. Pain and Suffering in the Light of Survival

Even philosophy has to consider the possibility, and even
the probability, that a human being does not stop existing at the
moment of death, that a person may survive forever. Examined
in the light of such everlasting survival, any kind of earthly
suffering, however strongly it may grip our emotion, loses
much of its significance. If the human person survives, it should

not be difficult for God to compensate overabundantly for any pain and suffering which he might have allowed the person to undergo during this life. The philosopher as such does not speak with great assurance in this field: the evidence is not convincing. Yet a strong case may be made for eternal survival, strong enough, it seems to me, to eliminate one of the horns of the famous dilemma "if God is infinitely good, he must wish to do away with all physical evil."[24]

We may put it another way: It seems that pain and suffering as we sometimes meet them cannot be reconciled with the existence of an omnipotent and good God, because when we speak of omnipotence and of goodness, we necessarily think on a human scale. We have the impression that if "we" were omnipotent and good, we would not allow all this suffering. We might be right in this. But it cannot so easily be shown that this suffering contradicts the existence of someone who is *infinitely* powerful and *infinitely* good, because whatever is infinite is for our mind an unfathomable mystery.

But this brings up an obvious objection. It goes somewhat like this. You claim that God's existence must be admitted because without it we cannot explain finite reality. You accuse those who reject your explanation and settle for an indefinite series of causes, as a sufficient explanation, of a lack of respect for the demands of their own intellect. But when their intellect demands an explanation for the appalling amount of pain which fills our earth, you tell them that this is a mystery which they cannot expect to understand. You are obviously using a double standard.

A first answer to this objection might be that I arrive at God, not as the explanation of the universe, but as the one whom I cannot not coaffirm in every one of my affirmations. This may be another reason why the transcendental way of establishing God's existence may be preferable to the usual cosmological or teleological proofs. For they arrive at God as the explanation of the universe or of its harmonious operation.

But they are unable to explain the presence of evil, of some kind of evil at least. My transcendental approach too is unable to do so. But it has not been presented as an explanation of the universe.

A second answer insists upon the need of an option. Human reason is unable to find a total answer for the problem of evil. Two extreme attitudes are possible in the presence of this basic difficulty. This first one claims that there is no explanation and that this absence of explanation invalidates all attempts to establish the existence of God. The other one asserts that there *must be* an explanation, but that it is hidden in the mystery of the Infinite Being.

The second attitude presents considerable advantages when it is compared with the first one. It explains all the goodness present in the universe and much (although not all) of the evil in it, whereas the first attitude explains nothing whatsoever. Moreover, the second attitude may eventually lead to a total explanation. The philosopher who adopts it, through some option of basic confidence, will not stop once he has admitted the existence of an Infinite Being. He will try to find out more about this being: he will listen in himself or in history whether this being has not spoken, and should he discover that there is solid proof that the Infinite has indeed spoken, he will accept this message with gratitude. True, this is no longer philosophizing; this is an act of faith, but one which looks very much like an authentic prolongation of the philosophical quest. This act of faith will eventually lead the philosopher who is willing to make it to the stunning discovery that the Infinite Being himself has assumed "catastrophic evil." That is the meaning of the crucifix, the only satisfactory answer to the problem of physical evil. If God himself has to such an extent undergone this kind of evil, it must have a meaning and it must make sense.

Most philosophers will demur in the presence of this obtrusion of theology into philosophy. And rightly so. This is no longer pure philosophy. I have forewarned them in the introduction that natural theology, as I understand it, makes sense only within an attitude of faith, that it is the *intrastructure* of theology. It is like a tenon. A tenon makes sense only within a mortise. The mortise here is faith or theology. Philosophers as philosophers have a perfect right to refuse the option for faith. I am not sure that, as human beings, they have that right. This is precisely where the humble, patient, trusting acceptance of pain and suffering may have an important function. As Blondel wrote: "To him who has felt a desire for the infinite, who is aware of the needs of conscience, but who has not wholeheartedly entered this narrow path of dying to life, which we have shown to be the only road of a logical will, revelation, although it may be awaited and desired, remains closed, scandalous, worthy of hatred, when it is not what he would expect it to be.[25]

7. The Essence of God according to Modern Philosophies

AGAINST THE TRADITIONAL DOCTRINE of the nature of God, as briefly explained above, serious objections have been presented and are being urged more and more nowadays. I feel it my duty to consider some of them.

The difficulties come from human reason, which receives the impression that there are contradictions in what it believes to be able to discover about God. They come also, and much more so, *from revelation,* from those who claim that God has spoken and told them many things about himself. I have not used revelation or faith in order to establish that God exists. But I have a right to listen to the difficulties which those who believe bring up against the conception of divine nature which seems to follow from the way I claim to arrive at its existence, especially when these difficulties tend to agree with those that come from reason.

We have already met some of these difficulties when we tried to reconcile divine omniscience and divine providence with the freedom of the human will. Another great source of difficulties is God's immutability. This attribute seems to follow in inexorable logic from God conceived as the infinitely perfect being. Yet it spawns quite a number of serious problems. God is immutable; he cannot change; he cannot be affected by anything distinct from him. He is not related to the world or to humanity. How can this be reconciled with other truths we affirm, with other things we believe or feel? How can an immutable God be said to be the creator of the universe? Even if we admit that creation, in God, is from all eternity (since he is not in time) and therefore implies no change, would God not be different from what he is now if he had not created? The same question arises in connection with the Incarnation. The christian professes that God became man. How can this be reconciled with an unchanging God? Can we really admit that, whether or not he becomes man, God does not change at all? Traditional theology squarely answers this question with Yes: when God becomes man, when he assumes a human nature, so it claims, there is absolutely no change in God; the only change occurs in the assumed human nature. Likewise the only difference between a creating and a noncreating God resides not in God but in the universe.

We hear that God is not related to the universe, to humanity, that he is in no way affected by anything that happens to them. If we spell this out more concretely, it means that whether people are good or wicked, happy or wretched, in no way affects God: it makes absolutely no difference to him. The frightful world wars, the Holocaust, the catastrophes that periodically affect a part of the world population, leave God totally indifferent. Humanity might have escaped these dreadful scourges, and what a difference it would have made for millions of hapless people! But to God it would have made no difference whatsoever!

This conception of God also robs human existence of any real significance, since it implies that if God had not created, if humanity had never existed, this would not take one jot away from the fullness of reality. It would have been all the same if there had been no evolution, no human history, no Covenant, no Incarnation.

The proponents of traditional philosophy might well at this point object that the above remarks smack of anthropomorphism. They would be right. When we say that something does not matter to God, does not affect him, leaves him totally indifferent, we are speaking of God as if here were a human being. The trouble is that when we call him unchangeable or immutable, not related or absolute, we act in the same way. If none of these terms strictly applies to God, if all of them have to be used analogously, why insist on immutability and unrelatedness? Why not rather say that God changes (analogously) and bears (analogously) real relations to his creatures?

One way out of these difficulties is, of course, to claim that the God of philosophy is not the same as the God of faith. I have explained above why this position is unacceptable. In that case it is not reasonable to believe: faith has no rational basis; it is wholly a matter of feeling, of taste. Faith makes sense only with an implicit or explicit philosophy of God as its intrastructure. This entails that what faith and theology tell us about God lies in the prolongation of what reason is able to discover about him.

When treating of the essence of God, I used the traditional philosophical approach. This is the approach of what is often referred to as the perennial philosophy, philosophy as it peaked in Aristotle and Aquinas, and also lived to a great extent in the works of Plato, Plotinus, Augustine, Descartes, Leibniz, and others. Now, among the basic notions of this philosophy are those of *being* and of *substance*, and its first principle is the principle *whatever is, is*.

Might we not reach a more acceptable conception of the nature of God by using other philosophies when we interpret what our intellectual dynamism tells us about God? Among these other philosophies there is, in this country, the process philosophy of A.N. Whitehead, who substitutes *becoming* to being and *process* to substance. And there is, coming from Germany, the philosophy of Hegel, for whom the first principle is trite, a mere tautology, and who attaches much more importance to what might be called the *principle of universal correlativity*: "Everything is itself by being related to something else."

Both these philosophies are impossible to explain briefly. I do not intend to do so, any more than I tried to explain the traditional philosophy I have used above in investigating the nature of God. I cannot accept these philosophies in their totality. Whitehead tells me that I am a "society of actual entities." I prefer to consider myself an individual and a person. Whitehead's God is finite, unconscious, and he stands at the service of some higher creativity. I cannot reconcile this with what my intellectual dynamism tells me about God. A conscious, infinite God, one whose creativity coincides with himself, corresponds better to the infinitely perfect being whom my intellect and my will forever keep intending. My main objection to Hegel is that he seems to teach that God creates the universe necessarily, because *he needs it* to be really God. This "needy" God stands lower than a God who, if he creates, does so freely out of the superabundance of his love.

So there can be no question of adopting these systems in their totality. But it might be possible to borrow from them some elements that might allow us to speak more acceptably about the nature of God.

A. God in Process Philosophy: Panentheism

Whitehead's system is too complicated and uses a vocabulary too technical to be useful for my purpose. I shall settle therefore for one of his most famous disciples, who is not a mere follower, but who has developed some of Whitehead's ideas in an original way, especially as they apply to the nature of God. I mean Charles Hartshorne.[1] There are, says Hartshorne, three views about the relation of God to the universe. "1) God is merely the cosmos, in all aspects inseparable from the sum or system of dependent things or effects; 2) he is both this system and something independent of it; 3) he is not the system, but is in all aspects independent."[2] The first of these conceptions represents *pantheism*. The second one is known under the name of *panentheism*. The third one is traditional *theism*, as briefly outlined above. Since theism includes about the nature of God positions which are more and more difficult to accept, we turn toward another way of conceiving God's relation to his creatures. Pantheism is unacceptable, because it does away with the transcendence of God and the freedom of man. But what about panentheism?

Panentheism holds that God both is and transcends the universe. The totality of created reality exists in him (*pan-en-theoi*: all-in-God), but he is more than this totality. This looks, at first blush, not different from the traditional doctrine when it claims that God is both immanent to the cosmos and transcendent with regard to it. However, panentheism claims not only that God is in the cosmos (immanent) but that the cosmos is in God. This again might be understood in a way that is quite traditional: God knows the universe and directs it, and therefore the universe is *in* the mind and *in* the power of God.

But panentheism goes further when it asserts that the universe is in God. For it the relation between God and the universe seems to resemble that which exists between my soul and my body: I am my body, but I am also more than it. God is the universe, but he is also more than it. In the same way in which I am influenced by the body which I am, God is influenced by the universe which he is. As a human person cannot exist in this world without a body, God cannot exist without the universe.

I have explained above why, according to traditional philosophy, only the pure perfections are to be found formally in God. As a result some qualities, which we greatly esteem in people around us, are denied of God, because they are mixed perfections that imply finiteness and potency. We like rich characters, with many harmoniously blended traits. Such a diversity in unity is excluded from God, because it is irreconcilable with his perfect simplicity. We like people who are both firm and adaptable, strong and receptive, energetic and sensitive. Traditional philosophy does not admit any adaptability, receptivity and sensitivity in God, because these qualities suppose that God is in potency, can receive and improve.

Thus it goes with most basic opposites: one and many, active and passive, cause and effect, eternal and temporal, substance and accident, necessary and contingent, absolute and relative. Theism admits the existence in God of only one of these contraries and claims that it exists in him in a way which goes beyond anything the human mind can conceive. Hartshorne's panentheism, on the other hand, admits that both contraries are realized in God and that they exist in him to the highest possible extent. Thus God would be supremely one, yet at the same time supremely multiple. He is supremely active and supremely passive or receptive. God is not only the infinite substance but he also possesses an infinite number of accidents. God, as a substance, is infinite, absolute, necessary, eternal, the cause of whatever exists. God, in his accidents, is finite, related to everything, contingent, in time, the effect of whatever happens.

Is it possible to arrive at the existence of such a God? We have tried to establish the existence of God by pointing out that the dynamism of our intellect keeps pointing toward the reality of a being who is infinitely perfect and absolutely necessary. Does infinite perfection and necessary existence include the fullest possible realization of all fundamental contraries? It is not easy to answer this question, because we have no adequate idea of infinite perfection and absolute necessity. We know them only by pointing toward them, by intending them. This, however, we know: if a perfection is seen by us as one than which a greater one may be conceived, it is not infinite. And it appears as if the mixed perfections, which panentheism puts in God, are such. At least this is the way in which theism sees it and has always seen it.

But Hartshorne and the panentheists put up a strong

defense. Absolute unity without any multiplicity means uniformity, monotony, poverty. It is an imperfection. Whatever we prize combines unity and diversity, a great unity with a rich diversity. Why should this not apply to God? A person who is only active, never passive or receptive, is a person devoid of all sympathy, of all compassion, is a ruthless and insensitive person. Such a person is called a tyrant. This is so in the case of the finite persons we know. Is it also true of an infinite person? Or is the need for diversity and receptivity not merely a consequence of finiteness? God might not have created. How could there be any need or even a possibility of receptivity in a noncreating God?

This question points to one of the typical features of panentheism. It applies only to a Creator God. Creation is necessary. God is not only himself but he is also the universe. Insofar as he is himself, he is infinite, absolute, necessary, one, pure act, universal cause, eternal. Insofar as he is universe, he is finite, relative, contingent, multiple, passive, universal effect, in time and in history.

Is this reconcilable with the idea of an infinitely perfect being? The answer to this question depends on the reason why God creates. If one says that God creates out of need, because without the universe he is not God, the answer can only be negative. A needy God cannot be an infinitely perfect God. On the other hand, if creation is a necessary effect of God's superabundant being and goodness, there seems to be no philosophical objection to the idea of a "necessary" creation. In this case, God is God even without the universe, although he never exists without it.

Thus some kind of panentheism might be acceptable. It does not identify the universe with God. God is distinct from the universe; the universe is distinct from him. God creates the universe, not out of need, but out of love. The universe is *in* God.

Since this statement "The universe is *in* God" is the

most typical one of panentheism, it deserves to be examined more thoroughly. What do we mean when we say that the universe is *in* God? Obviously it is not that God is the place in space, the location, where the universe may be found. This is the spatial meaning of *in*, which does not apply to God. We say more than that the universe is in God's knowledge and power. We say at least that between God and the universe there exist reciprocal relations. The universe is related to God, and God is related to the universe. Traditional theism never admitted this, because these relations would be accidents in God, to which his substance is in potency. It is true that we cannot help conceiving them in this way. But we realize that this, our way of conceiving these relations, does not correspond to reality. There is no potency in God. He does not need these relations to be himself (against Whitehead and Hegel). Far from deriving from any divine indigence, these relations originate from God's superabundant fullness and goodness. In this sense we might accept them and agree with panentheism.

When we say that the universe is in God, we also may mean that it is an interior modification and manifestation of God. That the universe is a manifestation of God is a traditional doctrine. That this manifestation is *interior* has to be understood in the same sense in which we understand the universe being *in* God. The universe may be called a *modification* of God, or at least something which implies a modification in God, in the sense that since the relations between him and it are reciprocal, there is a difference between a creating and a noncreating God. Although our mind forces us to think of such a modification as something to which God is in potency, we deny this way of "representing" the state of affairs; we "intend" or "mean" a modification which, far from being the actuation of a potency, is the result of a superactuality.

Panentheism understood in this sense differs from the one which is advocated by Hartshorne. As I understand him, Hartshorne holds that God creates necessarily, that he is not

God without creation, that he needs the universe to be really himself. I find this unacceptable, and I hold that God freely creates out of the superabundance of his love. He is, ontologically, if not chronologically, fully God before any creation. Hartshorne claims that in certain respects God is finite. He is supreme; he excells all other realities; he is unsurpassable. But he is not infinite in these respects; he keeps growing and in this way always surpassing himself. Against this I hold that God is in all respects actually infinite. Any growing and self-surpassing is undeniably a "passage from potency to act" that is totally inadmissible in the "whereunto" of our dynamism.

The difference between the panentheism of Hartshorne and the panentheism I tend to endorse might perhaps most clearly be expressed as follows: for the God of Hartshorne creation enriches, completes God, provides him with something he still needs. For me creation is a display, an unfolding of the infinite richness of the Fullness of Reality.[3]

A mitigated panentheism of this kind is being cautiously endorsed by some great christian thinkers. Thus, in his *Metafísica trascendental* Professor José Gómez Caffarena writes:

> From this point of view of the Absolute, the world, strictly speaking, is not. Since, however, *it is*, we must "locate" it *in* the Absolute. *It is* not the Absolute; *it is in* the Absolute. This way of putting it is shaky (*fragil*) and, of course, metaphorical. There is no question of any local "situation." . . . Yet it may well be the only one which is suggestive enough—provided one corrects the eventual misinterpretations—of this mysterious and unique relation. "God is in everything, or everything is in God." It is difficult to do without the panentheistic formula.[4]

Thus Maurice Blondel writes:

> And thus it is that a vision which stands at the other extreme of spinozistic pantheism will, without overlooking the

truths contained in this error, imply what has been called a "panentheism" that is totally opposed to monism, since, far from confusing the one and the all, it takes as its slogan, when speaking of this transcendent that gives itself without ceasing to belong to itself in its incommunicable perfection: *Omnia omnibus factus*.[5]

And Karl Rahner writes as follows:

> This form of pantheism does not simply identify the world with God in monistic fashion (God, the "All"), but sees the "All" of the world "within" God as an interior modification and manifestation of God, although God is not absorbed into the world.

And after having said what he thinks of this system as a theologian,[6] he continues:

> It is a demand that ontology undertake thinking out much more profoundly and much more accurately the relation which exists between absolute and finite being (that is, take into account the reciprocal conditioning of unity and distinction, as they grow in the same proportion).[7]

Traditional theism overemphasizes the distinction that exists between God and his creatures in the sense that by denying the reality of reciprocal relations between them it isolates God too much from the universe. Pantheism underemphasizes or suppresses the distinction between them, at least in the sense that it attributes to God a need for creating. God for the pantheist is not God without the universe. Between these two extremes an intermediary position is possible, one which admits that from God to his creatures the relations are reciprocal, (although, in God, not essential), while it denies that God needs the creatures to be himself. It claims that God creates, not out of any need of passing from being-in-himself to being-in-and-for-himself (Hegel), but only out of the superabundance of his love and the ensuing desire to share his fullness.

The God of this kind of panentheism is infinite self-consciousness in and by himself, without having to step outside of himself in creation (against Whitehead, Hartshorne and Hegel). He is by himself infinite perfection; nothing accrues to him from the universe, which he creates freely out of love. This kind of panentheism emphasizes God's love and generosity. It goes far beyond Aristotle, whose God does not love his creatures, does not even know them. Christian revelation tells us that God is love. Does reason tell us anything of the kind?

Blondel answers: it does. Here is what (as a philosopher) he has to tell us about divine love in one of his later works:

> What is irrational is to make of reason alone the measure of God and that of man himself. We had already remarked that, above the merely rational, the intelligible demands that the absolute Being should not be pure contemplation, through an evanescent return of cold thought upon motionless Thought . . . .[8]

The distinction which Blondel makes here between the *rational* and the *intelligible*, between *reason* and *intelligence*, corresponds to the one I made above between understanding and intellect. A similar distinction was made by St. Thomas, by Hegel and by other philosophers. Blondel's *reason* is our workaday knowing power as we use it in combination with sense knowledge. Intelligence tries to go beyond the obvious and the perceptible into the realm of the pure intelligible. It will use analogy and dialectics, which combine what may look like contradictory statements. When Blondel speaks of "pure contemplation, through an evanescent return of cold thought upon motionless Thought," he is alluding to Aristotle's God, the self-contemplating contemplation. Aristotle mentioned this sublime kind of knowledge as the highest activity of the Supreme Being. But he never mentioned love and generosity.

> Far from seeing the blending of a spiritual reality and of a generosity that goes all the way to a full giving away of itself, as

a depravation and as it were a childish image of the perfect Being, highest reason suspects in this burning hearth, if we may say so, the only *raison d'être* of Being and its incomparable dignity, its supreme value . . . .

In order to help to some extent our intelligence and imagination we may borrow a few traditional symbols, which, combined and despite the rectification which they call for, may serve to remove our misgivings and to enrich our outlook.

We wonder how creatures can arise there where metaphysically subsists that fullness of which, tied as he still was to material images, Parmenides gave us an impression with his perfect sphere, opaque and compact, outside of which there could only be illusion and inanity. This is where a spiritual image comes up, such as Ravaisson for instance had taken it over from St. Paul, to exult in this supreme invention of love, *Semetipsum exinanivit*.[9] Being has, as it were, withdrawn from part of its own fullness, has made a void in it, in order to put in it, not nothing, but that which would be able to render itself to itself . . . .

Some urge the difficulty of conceiving and justifying what we call a withdrawal and an "emptying" of God . . . . What incomprehension this bespeaks of the life of the spirit! For, if it is true that without goodness there is no spiritual reality, neither is there any goodness, without some kind of burdensome sacrifice, of personal abnegation, of an effort to uplift those to whom one gives oneself. God is eminently good: such is his being. He is such in his own and innermost generation; not in any *burdensome* way, to be sure, but with an altruism that is proof against all selfishness. He is such—although in another manner, and now, one might say, *with some risk*—in the creative work. For as he invites imperfect and fallible freedom to cooperate in his work, God runs the risk, so we are emboldened to say, of the partial failure of his will for universal salvation.[10]

And further on Blondel continues:

since we do not think without images and metaphors are un-avoidable, although they are only conditions, not the cause or the very essence of thought, let us use a system of symbols that will rid us of the misleading expressions which we have come to consider authentic metaphysical necessities. What do we usually imagine? Being is. Right. Yet, although we represent it to ourselves as full, even as the all, we cannot help putting beside it a nothingness, a void, in which it would be immersed or which it might envelop with its unimaginable extension.

Now, a few moments of reflection will show that this is an unacceptable materialization. Yet this is the error which has always haunted the mind of ordinary people and which, starting with Parmenides, more or less tyrannizes the most metaphysical speculation. How can we do away with this despotic and absurd representation?

Let us affirm that absolutely God leaves outside of himself absolutely nothing which we might imagine to be a void or call a positive nothingness. Where then shall we put the eventual or real creatures in this integrally compact monism? This is where metaphors that differ totally from the ones we criticized above may be useful. When, like Ravaisson, we used the sublime expression of St. Paul *Deus semetipsum exinanivit* (God has emptied himself), we had already mentioned that in order to create, God has not produced outside of himself a new *plenum*, or at least a *semiplenum*, an ontological nebula, something which would slowly have to coagulate so as to arrive physically at a solidification either material or spiritual. This is the false prestige of the senses which exposes us to speak in a bodily way of the invisible things themselves. It is less misleading to start from a wholly merciful intention of the Creator who makes ready, not in space, not in his substantial fullness, but in his fertile love, a capacity of life, of happiness, of transforming union for other himselves.[11]

My attention was called to these blondelian texts by Professor Louis Dupré's book *The Other Dimension*. In this connection Professor Dupré presents some ideas which might prove very useful. Thus he writes:

If God creates out of nothing, no thing can ever subsist apart from the creative act. To perceive the creature is to

> perceive the creative event. The creature is the divine act in its otherness. Creating means creating of otherness, but since the creative act is unconditioned, the otherness of the Creator remains within Him. Nothing can be detached from the living act, for outside the act no conditions exist to support created being.[12]

The creative activity is identical with God. It terminates in the creature. *Terminative*, it is the creature. The creature is, whatever it is, only on account of this creative activity. It is the other side of it. In that sense the creature may be called *God's otherness*.[13] In other words, if we look at the creative activity from God's side, it is identical with him. If we look at it from the creature's side, it is the creature. Yet God is not the creatures, nor are the creatures God. God "others" himself in them: they are God's otherness. As Professor Dupré puts it in a striking formula, "The creature is the total otherness of God within the total dependence upon God."[14]

In this sense it seems that we might say with the panentheists that God is both himself and not himself. He is also not himself, because he is the otherness of the creatures. Against Whitehead, Hartshorne and Hegel I insist that God is such, not by a necessity of his nature, but as a result of his infinite goodness. But with that proviso I am willing to say, with the panentheists, that God, as he is in himself, is one, absolute, necessary, immutable, eternal, and that God, as he is in the otherness of his creatures, is multiple, relative, contingent, changeable, in time and in history.

B. Can Hegel Help Us?

Early in this book I explained why I would not study the philosophy of God historically. I have made a few exceptions to this rule. A few words have been said about Aristotle's and Plato's conceptions of God. More time was spent listening to the view on God of St. Thomas Aquinas and of Kant. There is one more giant of human thought whom I cannot ignore. He is G. F. W. Hegel (1770-1831). There are many reasons for devoting some space to him. First, he may well be the most influential thinker of modern times. Moreover his whole gigantic philosophical system centers around God.[15] His two main works are the *Phenomenology of the Spirit* and the *Logic*. The former leads up to God; the latter is entirely devoted to a study of the Absolute. Hegel emphasized the close bond between the philosophy of God and man's religious faith in God. Like Spinoza, whom he admired, he might be called "God-intoxicated." Of him Maréchal wrote, "In Hegel himself, in spite of his plainly marked element of rationalism, we may recognize a mysticism of 'becoming divine'—a becoming which is at the same time begun and completed in the rational progression developed in the *Logic*."[16]

On the other hand, very much against what he may have wished and expected, he became the fountainhead of the most virulent forms of atheism, since through the left-wing hegelians he opened the way to Marxism, communism and atheistic humanism.

He is among all philosophers one of the most difficult to understand and practically impossible to explain briefly and clearly. For Hegel perhaps more than for any other great thinker a simplified summary turns into a caricature. An added difficulty comes from the fact that even among the philosophers who have studied him most thoroughly many disagreements exist about the way he should be interpreted. So I shall not attempt to explain or to summarize his system.

Yet Hegel is a thinker whom we cannot afford to ignore, because so many of his insights are as valuable as they are profound, and whom we cannot follow to the end, because somewhere along the line he seems to deviate from what I consider to be the truth. Of him Karl Barth said that he was "a great question mark, a great disappointment, yet perhaps also a great promise."[17] I will say a few words about these deviations, because they allow me to set forth my own position more sharply and to pay deserved attention to the positive contributions which enrich our philosophy of God.

Among the deviations the most fateful is that Hegel seems to be a pantheist in the strict sense of the word. Many Hegel scholars admit this; others strongly deny it; still others are undecided. Hegel himself has always denied it, but his denial is not convincing, because by pantheism he understands a doctrine which affirms that everything is God, and this Hegel does not admit; or the doctrine which, like Spinoza's, calls God the unique substance and considers all creatures as evanescent modes of God. Hegel, although an idealist, did not quite deny the reality of the universe.

For me, however, a pantheist in the strict sense of the word is a philosopher who claims that God needs creatures to be conscious of himself, to be truly God. Such a God creates necessarily, not freely, out of some indigence, not out of a superabundance of love. Here are a few texts of Hegel which seem to imply such a view.

> God is God only to the extent that he knows himself, and his self-knowing is, moreover, his consciousness of self in man.[18]

> Thus the finite is shown to be an essential moment of the Infinite; and if we posit God as the Infinite, he cannot, in order to be God, do without the finite.
> *Without world God is not God.*[19]

Hegel agrees with the following words of Meister Eckhart:

> The eye with which God sees me is the eye with which I see him . . . my eye and his eye are one . . . . If God were not, I would not be; if I were not, God would not be.[20]

> Thus we see that the *Weltgeist* (the world-spirit) has finally succeeded in getting rid of every extraneous objective

essence and in grasping itself as absolute Spirit . . . . The struggle of finite consciousness with absolute consciousness, that seemed to be external to itself, comes to an end. Thus finite consciousness has ceased to be finite, and thereby, on the other hand, *infinite consciousness has reached the reality it did not have before*.[21]

Let me add, for fairness' sake, that the Hegel scholars who claim that Hegel is no pantheist know these texts and do not draw the same conclusion from them. They hold that within the total context of his philosophy these texts do not imply strict pantheism.[22]

My personal opinion (which is not that of a Hegel scholar) tends to agree with the conclusion of a lengthy study of Professor Franz Grégoire devoted precisely to the problem which concerns us here: Is Hegel a pantheist, and if he is, in what sense is he? Here is his conclusion:

> Hegel keeps repeating that God is spirit. What does this mean basically, according to the interpretation which we tend to prefer? In reality, God is not distinct from the finite spirits, . . . insofar as they realize their essence and to the extent in which they do it. In this sense God is the totality of the finite spirits, or rather their system, i.e. the spirits grouped in different religions and different philosophies, dialectically interconnected. More specifically, the spirits attached to christianity, and even more specifically, the spirits who have accepted absolute idealism. But we must emphasize that the supreme essence of which all spirits are, in their own way, at their own level and through their ordered totality, the realization, that this essence is *unique*, and that *it posits through itself* its realizations, or, if one prefers, its total realization. It is a unique essence that posits its multiple empirical but organically structured reality.
>
> A pantheism that attributes the primacy to thought, that considers thought, in some form or other, as the foundation and the end of things, is an idealistic pantheism. The fact that it reduces thought to human thought makes it even more strictly

pantheistic. Hence, Hegel's system is an eminently pantheistic idealistic pantheism.[23]

And again:

> The Absolute Idea is a unique center of thought, lacking personal consciousness, constituting both the substratum and the cause of the universe. In other words, a real, tendencial and active virtuality of the universe, totally relative to it, and which is primordially a virtuality of absolute Spirit.[24]

I agree with the defenders of Hegel when they claim that their master did not want to be a pantheist. But I also agree with those who, while admitting this, assert that the great German philosopher's system led him into pantheism. Thus Professor Henri Rondet seems to be right when he writes:

> Although Hegel tries very hard to uphold God's transcendence, does he not confine him within the limits of the universe that proceeds from him? Finally, even if one keeps in mind how extremely difficult it is to express "speculatively" the relation of God and the world and if one inclines therefore to be indulgent for a philosopher whose formulas perhaps betray his intuition, other questions come up. [25]

1. The first among these other questions is the way in which Hegel understands the relation between religion and philosophy. For him these two supreme productions of the human spirit have the same content; they differ only in the way in which they present it. Religion presents it on the level of understanding, by means of "representations"—that is, of imaged thoughts—whereas philosophy presents it on the level of reason, in pure concepts, without undue immixture of imagery. Religion would thus be the ordinary person's philosophy, a makeshift for those who cannot reach the level of philosophy. It is true that Hegel admits that religion keeps its value even for the philosopher. The philosophical stance is not an easy or a natural one, since it consists in a reflection on ordinary experience. Nobody, not even the professional philosopher,

can permanently remain on this reflective level. In everyday life even he will approach the divine reality in the natural way, through religion.

The following quotations, from a leading Hegel scholar, will show why Hegel's conception of the relation between faith and philosophy presents real problems. According to Hegel, says Professor Fackenheim,

> Christian faith *finds* the Christian totality; philosophical thought *demonstrates* its totality and transforms representational fact into speculative necessity.[26]

> For Christian faith, the ripeness of the time for Christ, brought about by the meeting of Jewish East and Greek-Roman West, is a contingent fact. For speculative thought, it is an inner, self-developing necessity.[27]

> Hegel's work therefore culminates in the transfiguration of the Christian comprehensive Truth, accepted as fact by faith, into speculative necessity.[28]

If, as it has been argued in behalf of Hegel's position, philosophy is but an effort to think through the content of one's faith, it is difficult to see how it differs from theology. But philosophy is the most autonomous of all sciences, attaches no importance to testimony, whereas theology is based on the testimony of God as it comes to us from revelation and the teaching of the church. There is, of course, a way out of this difficulty. If God's testimony does not come to us from outside, through revelation and tradition, if he speaks directly to our mind, if he thinks in us, there would be no more heteronomy. But can this still be called *faith*? Yet this is what Hegel seems to have had in mind according to Professor Fackenheim: "What for Christian faith is free reception of the Divine by the human is for speculative thought divine activity in the human."[29]

"For Christianity the comprehensive Truth which it accepts in faith, drops from heaven. For philosophic comprehension, it is the end of a process which must begin with the lowest if it is to reach the highest.''[30] The philosopher follows the human spirit as it develops a succession of religions and philosophies that become more and more spiritualized. He begins with the lowest and eventually reaches the highest, to discover gradually the essential mysteries of the christian faith.[31] For Hegel the revealed christian religion is "the comprehensive truth of all religions.''[32] The ordinary christian receives it from outside, through the testimony of the church, which one accepts in faith. Even the philosopher may do this in everyday life. But when one reflects as a philosopher, faith no longer "drops from heaven." It is the result of his own reflection as he works his way through the long history of mankind's religious thought. "The revealed religion must be the comprehensive religion: indeed, it will emerge that 'comprehensive' is what 'revealed' means.''[33] This is the way in which Hegel's system "culminates in the transfiguration of the Christian comprehensive Truth, accepted by faith, into speculative necessity.''[34] There is no doubt that Hegel's philosophy of religion is a powerful mental construction, but there seems also to be no doubt that it does away with real religious faith.

2. For Hegel God is spirit, and the universe is his idea. This is, in a certain sense, a traditional conception, provided we center the universe exclusively in God. Hegel centers it also in the human mind, which in his view coincides to a great extent with the divine mind. I cannot accept this. It is true that the human mind shares some of God's knowledge, but in a very humble way. We stand, not at the center of reality with God, but on a sideline. We look at it "eccentrically"; we have to make a correction for the resulting parallax. That is why our knowledge of the supreme realities has to use analogy. Hegel admits that our *understanding* needs and uses analogical knowledge,[35] but he claims that our *reason* can do without it and directly grasp the fullness of truth.

God knows reality by producing it. Since he puts the divine Spirit within the human spirit, Hegel lets man too produce the universe, with the Absolute who thinks in and through the human spirit. It seems to conform more to the truth to say that man in his thinking does not produce but to some extent "reproduces" the universe by using to this end some a priori knowledge directly deriving from God (metaphysics) and the a posteriori knowledge that comes from sense experience.

3. Hegel writes: "Man knows God only insofar as God knows Himself in man. This knowledge is God's consciousness of self, but at the same time it is God's knowledge of man: and this knowledge of man by God is man's knowledge of God."[36] Professor Quentin Lauer comments, "The thought which thinks infinity is infinite thought, and infinite thought is the thought of God Himself."[37]

In a certain sense this is undeniable. The knowledge of the Infinite by the finite cannot be the work of the finite. If man knows the Infinite, there must be something infinite in him. But this is not necessarily an infinite thought, an infinite intellect, coinciding with that of God. It may be a finite intellect endowed with an infinite capacity. This infinite capacity of a person's finite intellect shows in the intellectual and voluntary dynamism which, by knowing or experiencing the limit as limit, tends beyond it without ever being able to "grasp" the Infinite. Hegel's conception, as interpreted by Lauer, explains why human beings can think the Infinite. It does not seem to explain why their knowledge of the Infinite is hazy and shaky. Maréchal explains both the fact that one knows the Infinite (the intellect has an infinite capacity) and the fact that this knowledge is so deficient (the intellect is finite).

> Why should a finite intellect not be objectively infinite, that is, infinite as a capacity of objects? It is true that this blending of finite and infinite would be contradictory for every hypothesis but one . . . . This hypothesis supposes that finite and infinite are reconciled through the natural finality, through the basic tendency of the intellective power. A tendency which

is necessarily contingent as existence and finite as a subjective essence may, on the other hand, be infinite in its objective capacity and absolute in the necessity it imposes upon the becoming orientated by it. The objective capacity and necessity of a tendency are measured only by the range and the necessity of its ultimate end, while the existence and subjective essence of it depend on conditions which are necessarily limiting and contingent.[38]

At this point my reader may well wonder why we should bother with Hegel if his ideas about God and religion are so wide off the mark. The reason why we should bother with him is that no philosopher has probed more profoundly into the very difficult problem of the relation that exists between the Infinite and the finite. Hegel wanted to solve this problem without getting into pantheism. It looks very much as if the trend of this thinking forced him unwillingly into this error. But this is no reason to jettison all his ideas. Even those who hold him to be a pantheist admit that many of them are very profound and fruitful. Why not salvage and use them? Why not try to do with Hegel what Maréchal did with Kant and Fichte? Hegel is one of the most profound thinkers of all times. It would be unwise to ignore his insights.

I mentioned above that Hegel attaches scant importance to the principle of identity (Whatever is, is—A is A). He claims that this principle is tautological and trite, that it is the first principle of human understanding, not of human reason. The latter's basic, or first, principle is, according to Hegel, "A is both A and not-A," or "Whatever is is both identical with itself and not-identical with itself." At first sight this principle is difficult to manage for common sense and traditional philosophy. Yet if with one great Hegel scholar we interpret it as I shall presently explain, the principle seems to make sense. When, according to Professor Franz Grégoire, Hegel says that A is not-A, he means that A is itself only on account of its relation to not-A. There is, continues Professor Grégoire, no domain where the principle of identity (everything is itself) and the principle of not-contradiction (everything is distinct from that which is not itself) do not apply. We should rather say that, taken in their everyday, undeniable and empty meaning, these two principles apply to everything. But they must be *completed* and *rendered more precise* by means of a higher principle, the principle of universal correlativity (everything is itself precisely by being related to something else).

Between the principles of identity and noncontradiction lies a third principle,

which states that everything has to be itself and not-itself, to be itself precisely as not-itself, as essentially related to that which is other than itself. This principle does not destroy the initial principles; it *transposes* them. It does not simply state that something is itself by being purely and simply not-itself. But it brings about a *higher union* between the very general idea of something *being itself* (affirmed by the principle of identity) and the very general idea of something *being not-itself* (denied by the principle of noncontradiction) under the guise of the idea of something being itself as related to what is not-itself.[39]

Interpreted in this way, the principle that A is both A and not-A is understandable. But it is difficult to see that it is a basic principle. A basic principle is one that is a condition of the possibility of every affirmation, one which we affirm in the very act of denying it. It is easy to show that the principle of identity fulfills these conditions. I do not see how the principle of universal correlativity does.

Someone may object, however, that the principle of universal relativity is, in fact, coaffirmed in every one of our affirmations. Here is why. We can affirm something only by using concepts and words. But concepts and words—or better, concepts as expressed in words—have come to us from others, from the non-I. In this sense the non-I is presupposed by every one of my affirmations. The affirmation of the non-I is a condition of the possibility of my thought: whenever I affirm something, whenever I perform a human action (which always implies an affirmation), I assert the fact that I am related to others. I affirm the principle of relativity.

There is some truth in this objection. However, my relationship to others is an *ontic* precondition, not a *transcendental* precondition, of my affirmations and my actions. And only transcendental preconditions of my judgments may be considered basic, undeniable certitudes. An ontic precondition is one "whose existence is presupposed to make an activity possible, but which is not itself a part of this activity nor coaffirmed by it."[40] A transcendental precondition, on the other hand, is one which is coaffirmed in the very judgment which it renders possible, so that he who denies it contradicts himself, at least implicitly. Like the ontic precondition it is a condition of the possibility of the judgment. But, unlike the ontic precondition, it is not merely presupposed, it is also, although unthematically, coaffirmed in the affirmation.[41] Thus, the principle of identity is both presupposed and implicitly coaffirmed in every judgment. On the other hand, my dependence on the finite non-I, although undoubtedly presupposed, is not coaffirmed in every judgment, anymore than is the existence of food and oxygen that are also presupposed by every one of my affirmations and of my actions.

There is no doubt, however, that the principle of relativity seems to apply to all the beings of our experience. I am myself by being related to what is not myself, to other people, to the world, to God. The same applies to all other finite beings. Our question is: Does it apply to God? Can we say of him that "he is himself precisely by being related to something else"? Certainly not, if by this "something else" we mean creatures, the universe. This is one of Hegel's positions which is unacceptable. It would apply only to a God who would *need* the creatures to be really himself.

The principle could be acceptable for God if it were stated as follows: "Everything that exists is related to something else." Such a relation is true of creatures, because they need it to be themselves. It is true of God, because he freely assumes it out of his superabundant love.

Therefore the principle of universal correlativity, as we find it in Hegel, does not apply to God. This becomes even more evident if we consider what the principle means in the opinion of Professor Grégoire. It "states that everything has to be itself and not itself, to be itself precisely as not itself, as essentially related to that which is other than itself." I am unwilling to admit that God is himself precisely as not himself, as essentially related to that which is other than himself. God is himself in and by himself. He does not become himself or more himself in the otherness of his creatures. He is related to his creatures *not essentially*, not in such a way that without this relation he is not God. He is related to them, if I may use this word, "supereffluently," because the superabundance of his love leads him to share with them the fullness of his being.

It follows that we can accept Hegel's famous definition of God, although not precisely in the sense in which he himself understood it. God, says Hegel, is the Identity of Identity and non-Identity. God is Himself (Identity); he is also not-Himself: he is the otherness of his creatures (non-Identity). And he is the Identity of these two "aspects": Identity of Identity and non-Identity.

But in Hegel's view God needs the non-Identity to be really himself, to reach Identity. This I deny. He is totally, fully himself by and in himself. He freely assumes the non-Identity of creation. The definition is not acceptable in the pantheistic sense, which seems to be Hegel's sense; it may be acceptable in the panentheistic sense explained above.

C. Theological Excursus

Hegel's example, however—not to speak of that of medieval philosophers, such as St. Bonaventure, or modern ones, such as Blondel—might allow us to have a look at some data of christian revelation and to see whether Hegel's basic principle applies to them. We are told in scripture that God is one in nature and three in persons. He is one and not one, three and not three. We are told that the divine persons are subsisting relations. The Father is himself precisely by being related to the Son and to the Spirit. I hold, with Karl Rahner, that the Infinitely Perfect and necessarily existing Being, for whose existence I have tried to make a case in reason, is not some common divine nature, shared by the three persons; it is the Father, the fountainhead of the Trinity and of all reality. It follows that the "whereunto" of our intellectual dynamism that we know through our reason is a being who is himself only by being related to another one. But we are unable to discover this by reason alone.

With Prof. Grégoire I have interpreted Hegel's basic principle "A is A and not-A" in the sense that A is A only by being related to not-A. It is doubtful, however, whether Hegel always understood it in this weaker meaning. He often took it in its full, obvious sense. It is a remarkable fact that in this stronger sense the principle seems to include many of the truths which christians learn from revelation. God is one, and God is three. God is immutable, but he becomes man. Christ is God, and Christ is man. Traditional theological reflection on these two last statements tried to reconcile them with a strict immutability of God by claiming that when God became man in the Incarnation, there was no change in God, the change occurred only in the human nature that God assumed.

But a great modern theologian who is also an outstanding philosopher no longer admits this explanation. Here is what he says:

> God can become something, he who is unchangeable in himself can *himself* become subject to change *in something else* . . . . This "changing *in* another" must neither be taken as denying the immutability of God in himself nor simply

reduced to a changing *of* the other . . . . The immutability of
God is a dialectical truth like the unity of God . . . we learn
from the incarnation that immutability (which is not eliminated)
is not simply and uniquely a characteristic of God, but that in
and in spite of his immutability *he* can truly *become* something.
He himself, he, in time. And this possibility is not a sign of
deficiency, but the height of his perfection, which would be less
if in addition to being infinite, he could not become less than he
(always) is. This we can and must affirm, without being
Hegelians. And it would be a pity if Hegel had to teach
Christians such things.[42]

And elsewhere he returns to the same theme:

With respect to the immutability and the atemporality of
God christian theology should keep in mind the dogma of the
true Incarnation and temporalization of the Logos and not make
her task easier than it is. She will maintain the dogma of the
"immutability" and of the "eternal" atemporality of God "in
himself," but she will at the same time have to say that, in the
otherness of world history, God *himself* experiences change and
therefore time, that the world's time is his own history. As the
eternal he does not only creatively posit time, but he also freely
assumes it as his own determination.[43]

Both these texts obviously assume that God is himself and
God is also the other, since he is said really to change, he
himself, not, however, in himself, but in the other. How could
God himself change in the other unless he were the other?
Applying this to a truth which we derive from philosophy, we
may then also say that when God creates, he himself changes,
not in himself, but in the other, in the cosmos which he creates.

But is this not pantheism? It is not in the strict sense
because God is also the other not out of need, not because he has
to be the other in order to be fully himself. He is the other
because of the overflowing superabundance of his goodness,
which freely shares and cannot not share with the other. Very
apposite in this connection are the following remarks of another
philosopher-theologian:

Therefore the living christian God is a God who does not exclude, but who includes his antithesis. Not, as Greek metaphysics would have to suppose, because he stands in need of it, not by way of an initial stage, which would have to be completed in self-development, but as gracious power, as positive "possibility" which belongs from the start to his full reality.[44]

And again,

God's incarnation can never be deduced. God does not divest himself in his Word and Son because the hour has struck in world history or in his own divine life. He divests himself—we can never insist enough on this—out of his free grace. Hence it is not because he is in potency that he sets himself in motion; it is not because he needs it that he changes; it is not because he is imperfect that he becomes. To believe such things would make of God a copy of human wretchedness. If we wish to think christologically within the framework of greek metaphysics, we would rather have to say: it is precisely because God is Pure Act, superabundant fullness, immutable perfection, because he is the exalted God and not a creature, that he can undergo in his Word and Son such a self-emptying, without losing himself, that he can enter worldly mutability without giving up his immutable divine perfection, that he can afford this seemingly godless descent into the depths without miserably perishing in this transition into otherness. God can do all this; he does not have to do it. And although he does not have to do it, he wills it, once more out of the supereffluent superabundance of his gracious love, which wishes to identify itself with Man and his fate in this world.[45]

D. Panentheism—Summary

From the preceding discussion we may draw the following conclusion. An intermediate position is possible between traditional theism and pantheism. The former overemphasized the distinction between God and his creatures, especially by rejecting between them any reciprocal relations. The latter, by minimizing the distinction too much, detracted from the being both of God and of his creatures, especially the reasonable ones: of God by claiming that he needs creation in order to be fully himself; of the creatures, by denying their real autonomy.

We might have called this intermediate position *panentheism* if this term had not been preempted by Hartshorne. It is panentheism because it "sees the All of the World 'within' God as an interior modification and manifestation of God, although God is not absorbed into the world" (Rahner). 'Within' is, of course, a term that does not apply to God in the spatial sense. It means that between God and his creatures some relations are reciprocal; it means that creatures are in God as God's otherness, that God is both himself and, in his creatures, other than himself.

Some readers may feel like going part of the way in the suggested direction, but not quite all the way. They admit that between God and the universe some relations are reciprocal, because they understand that relations which are freely assumed out of love, far from being a sign of indigence and dependence, are a manifestation of power. But they do not see why we should say that the universe is within God except if this expression means nothing more than the presence of the above-mentioned reciprocal relations, in which case it seems preferable to them to eschew this terminology. And why should we add that the universe is an interior modification and manifestation of God, that the universe is God's otherness?

My answer is that all these expressions only make more explicit what is implied once we admit some reciprocal relations between God and the universe. Let me show this for each of the disputed statements. *Interior modification and manifestation*: Like 'within' the term 'interior' should not be taken in any spatial sense. God is not in space; he has no extension. Interior implies only reciprocal relations, but it emphasizes the fact that God is much more intimately connected with his creatures than traditional theism, out of fear for pantheism, is willing to admit. *Modification*: the reciprocity of the relations, especially of the creative relation, implies that there *is* a difference between a creating and a noncreating God. *Manifestation*: creation manifests the superabundance of love and goodness of the Creator. I have already explained above in what sense *the universe is God's otherness*. God *is* his creative activity. Through this activity God is related to his creature. God is one term of the relation; the creature is *the other* one. Might we not in this sense say that the creature is the otherness of a divine activity, therefore the otherness of God himself?

This kind of panentheism makes it possible to avoid some serious difficulties which have always dogged traditional theism. We are no longer forced to claim that there is no difference whatsoever (except in our mind) between a creating and a noncreating God. We no longer have to hold that God is in no way affected by what happens to his creatures. Traditional theism had to admit that whether they are good or wicked, happy or miserable, makes no difference whatsoever to God. For this kind of theism it is all the same to God whether or not he created, whether or not he made a covenant with man, whether or not he became a human being through the Incarnation. It has to hold that a God who is immutable could not in any way be influenced by his creatures. In stronger language we would say: Such a God does not care for his creatures, has no love for them. For how could God care for and love beings with which he has absolutely no relation? In fact, it would seem that this kind of theism would be more logical if it took over most of Aristotle's philosophy of God. Aristotle claimed not only that God does not love his creatures but also that he does not know them. It is not easy to see how a God who knows his creatures does not have a real cognitive relation to them.

It seems also easier to reconcile God's omniscience and human freedom in this system. For we may now admit that God knows from all eternity my future free decisions, because I will freely perform them. The older theism could not admit this, since it implies some influence of the creature upon the Creator.

The problem of physical evil too finds somewhat more of an answer in this conception. If the universe is in God, it is to him somewhat as our body is to us; the suffering too is in him: he himself, in his otherness, has as it were freely assumed it, as he once assumed death in the otherness of the body of his Son.

Does this not entail that sin too is in God? It does not any more than the traditional doctrine that God is the cause of all beings entails that he is the cause of sin. As explained above, evil, both physical and moral, is not a being, but a privation of being. God is the cause of all beings, not of all privations of being. Likewise all beings are in God, but not all privations of being.

E. Transcendence and Immanence

One of the most difficult problems of the philosophy of God is to explain how the divine transcendence can be reconciled with the divine immanence, how we must understand the relation that exists between the Infinite and the finite.

Here is the way in which Hegel puts the difficulty: If the Infinite and the finite are set over against each other,

> taken as *devoid of connection* with each other so that they are only joined by 'and', then each confronts the other as self-subsistent, as in its own self only affirmatively present. Let us see how they are constituted when so taken. The infinite, in that case, is *one of the two*; but as *only* one of the two it is itself finite, it is not the whole but only *one* side: it has its limit in what stands over against it; it is thus the finite infinite. There are present only *two finites*. It is precisely this holding of the infinite *apart* from the finite, thus giving it a *one-sided* character, that constitutes its finitude and, therefore, its unity with the finite. The finite, on the other hand, . . . is the same self-subsistence and affirmation which the infinite is supposed to be.[46]

The point is, of course, very well taken. No wonder that one leading theistic philosopher speaks of "la tremenda logica de esta dificultad."[47] We are in a real quandary. We cannot say that the Infinite and the finite are two, since this finitizes the infinite. And we cannot say that they are one, since this suppresses the finite or does away with the transcendence of the Infinite.

Hegel seems to settle for the latter solution. Here is how Professor Franz Grégoire summarizes his solution,

> The only way in which the finite's characteristic relation to the infinite is thinkable is that there corresponds to it an essential relation of the infinite to the finite. On the other hand and reciprocally the infinite on its own account is unthinkable without this same relation to the finite; it demands and contains the finite as such, the finite with its very finitude.[48]

I for one cannot accept Hegel's solution, which presents us a God who seems to need the finite to be himself. The dynamism of my intellect strives beyond such a God toward one who does not have such a need. It is difficult to avoid the impression that, despite his denials and the vigorous rejection of this conclusion by some of his followers, Hegel is a pantheist in the strict sense of the word.

But how then shall we answer the difficulty? Let me first present it again in a rather popular way, under the form of the following objection: God plus the universe is more than God alone. But to the Infinite nothing can be added. Therefore God is not infinite. To which I reply, in simple language too: God's infinity is not extensive or quantitative, but intensive. Intensities cannot be added in the way quantities can. You cannot add pink (a less intense shade of red) to scarlet. If you add the power of the secretary of state to that of the president of the United States, you do not increase the latter's power, because all the power of the former is but a less intense sharing of the president's power.

The power of both officials is real, yet they cannot be

added to each other. In the same way the world and God are both real, yet their being cannot be added. The real being of the world is but a sharing of God's being, a less intense form of it. Of course, the comparison does not apply perfectly. The president's power is shared by a person who exists in his own right, whereas in the case of the universe there is no previous recipient of the sharing; the very recipient exists only through the sharing. If I inquire whether the power of the secretary of state is his or the president's, the best answer seems to be: it is his. He exercises it; he makes the decisions, eventually the blunders; he is responsible. It is his power, although he received it from the president. He is a person who exists and operates to some extent independently of the chief executive. But when I ask Is the being of the universe really its being, or is it God's being? the answer is no longer so obvious. There is no previously existing independent agent that receives this being. It does not follow that the being of the universe must be considered as God's very being, but it follows that the distinction between the being of the universe and that of God is not as great as that which obtains between the power of the two officials.

This becomes even more obvious if we reflect upon the fact that the distinction between God and the universe is produced by God himself. It is a real distinction, and whatever is real is posited by God. As Karl Rahner puts it,

> The distinction between God and world is of such a kind that the former posits and is the latter's distinction from him, thus bringing about the greatest unity in the distinction. For if the distinction itself derives from God, is—so to speak—identical with God, then the distinction between God and world should be conceived in a way which wholly differs from the distinction between objects of our experience. In their case there exists a previous distinction, since they already presuppose in some way a space that shelters and distinguishes them. None of these empirically distinct realities posits or is the distinction that

distinguishes them from others. That is why we might call pantheism the feeling (better: the transcendental experience) that God is the absolute reality, the primordial ground, the ultimate whereunto of transcendence.[49]

God is certainly distinct from the world. But he is distinct in the way in which this distinction is given to us in our original transcendental experience. In this experience this remarkable unique distinction is experienced in such a way that the whole of reality is carried by and only becomes intelligible through this whither and this whence. Thus the distinction itself affirms once more the ultimate unity of God and the world and only in this unity is the distinction intelligible.[50]

When trying to explain the relation between God and world, we meet a difficulty which resembles the one we meet when speaking of body and soul. Body and soul are distinct; they are not one. Yet they are not two. Likewise God and the universe are not one. Yet they are not two. To say that they are two is to make both of them finite, is to say that something overarches them, of which both of them participate. Both of them would be a part of reality, of being. And this is false. God is reality, is being; he is *omnitudo realitatis,* the totality of reality. But what are we to say of the universe? It looks as if the only possible solution is to put it in God. That is precisely what panentheism does. It is an intermediate position between pantheism, which holds that God and the universe are one, and theism, *as it is often understood,* which holds that God and the universe are two.

The most authentic interpreters of traditional theism were well aware of these difficulties. They do not claim that God and the universe are two realities distinct in such a way that they may be added to each other. The distinction which they admit is that between the fullness of reality and that which participates in this fullness. They explain the relation between God and the world as one of participation. Participation includes several elements: it partakes of exemplary, efficient and final causality.

Plato, who explained material realities through their participation in the Ideas, insisted especially upon exemplary causality. Things on earth are modeled after their heavenly ideas. This conception was taken over by Aquinas, who put the ideas in God himself and added to it the reason why things are so modeled, why they were images of something else. God creates them according to his own creative ideas. Thus he combined efficient with exemplary causality. Now the image of the exemplary ideas, embedded in things, is their substantial form. It not only makes every reality into what it is but it also constitutes its inner finality, to dictate its end and direct its activities. In this way all creatures not only come from God, are made after his creative ideas, but they also tend to return to him as their ultimate end. To exemplary and efficient causality has been added final causality. Thus we see that the idea of participation is a very rich one. Yet even so it may not yet be rich enough to explain fully God's relation to his creatures.

The three kinds of causality which it employs are *extrinsic* causalities: the maker, the model and the end are distinct from the reality which they influence; they remain outside of it. That is why traditional theism has no qualms in using them to explain God's relation to his creatures. But do these extrinsic causalities sufficiently explain God's immanence in the creatures? Is it not possible to enrich the idea of participation with a certain amount of intrinsic causality? Here theism is wary, and not without good reason. The intrinsic causes are the material and the formal causes. To call God the material cause of things is sheer pantheism. And the same seems to be true if we call him, without further explanation, the formal cause of the universe. To say that God is the formal cause of the universe is to say that the universe is God's body, that he is to it as my soul is to my body. In some respects this comparison may be useful, but in many more senses it is misleading.

I have already mentioned one sense in which this idea might apply. Of God and the universe we may not say that they are two totally distinct realities, because this would make of God a part of reality and thus render him finite. On the other hand, we would also err if we said that God and the universe constitute only one reality. This would rob God of his transcendence, which is done in strict pantheism. Now the same difficulty faces us when we speak of soul and body. They are not two distinct substances, yet they are not to be identified with each other.

Here is another sense in which the comparison applies. The human soul is both immanent in the body and to some extent transcendent with respect to it. As a substantial form it is totally immanent in the body and makes it into a human body. As a spirit in matter it transcends the human body. The most typical feature of this transcendence is the dynamism of the human intellect and of the human will, both of which reach for infinity. The same is true for God: he is immanent in the universe, yet he infinitely transcends it.[51]

But there are many more respects in which the comparison does not apply. God creates the universe; the soul does not create the body. God is God without the universe; the soul is not a soul without a body, or, at least, without a transcendental, constitutive relation to matter. God operates in total independence of his creation; the soul is dependent on matter, intrinsically for many of its operations, extrinsically for all of them. There exists an interaction between soul and body, not that which occurs between two distinct things, but that which exists between the determining and the determined element, between the shape of a statue and its marble, between the meaning of a sentence and its words. Traditional theism rejects such an interaction and claims that God cannot be influenced by anything, that all relations between God and his creatures are unilateral.

We have seen that not only pantheism in the strict sense but also panentheism admits such an interaction. If the latter detracts from God's infinite perfection, it is unacceptable. But panentheism insists that it does not detract, since receptivity, sympathy, sensitivity, openness for the wishes and needs of others are essential ingredients of every real love. This is obviously quite true for all human love, for all finite love. Does it apply to infinite love? Since we have no adequate idea of infinite love, we cannot answer this question. It looks very much as if it did. The God of religion, the God of the Bible, is undoubtedly receptive, sensitive: he does care, he is attentive to our wishes, needs and prayers. But the Bible is often anthropomorphic. And it is not easy to fit these features into the picture which the philosophy of God draws of the Infinitely Perfect Being.

Therefore it is better to avoid using the image of soul and body to explain the relation of God to the universe. That relation is one of participation, and it seems that we must be satisfied with a combination of extrinsic kinds of causality—exemplary, efficient and final—to understand the idea of participation. Introducing any kind of formal causality into it leads into serious difficulties.

We might be tempted to speak of a quasi-formal causality of God with respect to his creation, in order to indicate that God's immanence in creation is not sufficiently stressed by the three above kinds of causality. By speaking of quasi-formal causality we would indicate that the divine immanence is more intimate than "participation," yet not as intimate as would be real formal causality. To speak in simpler terms, we would say that God is more than the modeler, the maker and the end of the creatures, yet less than their soul. The trouble is that the term 'quasi-formal causality' has been preempted by catholic theology to indicate the indwelling of God in the souls of the just through sanctifying grace. It is better therefore to avoid it and to conclude that we have no fitting term to express that most peculiar relation which creatures have to their creator. Our concepts derive ultimately from sense experience; they are not supple enough to grasp and express what towers infinitely above this experience. We must try to make do dialectically by mutually balancing affirmations and negations.

The philosophy of God presented in this book might have been called 'panentheism' if the term were not in this country so intimately connected with the work of Charles Hartshorne. Since I cannot accept the Hartshornian brand of panentheism, because it has overemphasized God's immanence at the expense of his transcendence, I prefer not to call my system panentheistic.

It is a form of theism. But it differs from the theism that is often presented in textbooks because it insists more than they do on God's immanence in the universe. Traditional theism is so anxious to safeguard the divine transcendence that it frequently undermines this very transcendence. By separating God too much from the universe it easily produces the impression that God and the universe are as totally distinct from each other as for example two human persons are. Then Hegel's famous objection assumes its full strength and is almost impossible to answer: "The infinite, in that case, is *one of the two*; but as *only* one of the two it is itself finite." That is why the theism which is presented here has taken over some ideas of panentheism. By insisting more on God's immanence I have tried to safeguard his utter transcendence. "There is," writes Professor J. Gómez Caffarena, "no final position that may be called *unequivocally* 'theistic' or *unequivocally* 'pantheistic'."

8. Atheism

MORE THAN EVER BEFORE in human history there are people who deny the existence of God: some quietly, implicitly, by ignoring him, by living as if he did not exist; others more forcefully, by voicing their denial.[1]

Atheism derives from many sources. Among them the three main ones may well be (1) the influence of science, (2) the problem of evil, and (3) the growth of humanism.

1. Before the advent of the sciences people explained most of the events they did not understand through a direct intervention of God. God caused rain and sunshine, famine and fertility. A few thousands of years ago he had directly made sun, moon and stars, plants, animals and men, as they still are today. We know how the theory of evolution thoroughly changed this conception and how the sciences were able to explain more and more of the things and occurrences that had always puzzled mankind. The need of God as an explanation kept diminishing, and the time seems not remote when everything on earth will be explained by science. Since science does not need God and can, as science, not lead up to him, quite a number of people with a scientific or positivistic turn of mind gave up the idea of God and their belief in his existence.

Of the many reasons why people become atheists this is one of the shallowest and most naive. The great theistic philosophers have never explained events on earth through a direct intervention of God. They have never made of him the first link in a chain of events. They knew that God does not, as a rule, act directly in the universe, but operates through secondary causes. He is not a categorial cause, but the transcendent creative cause. He actively keeps in being a universe which functions according to the laws he has given to it.

Atheists of this kind expect science to be able to explain everything; they do not notice that science cannot even explain itself. When a physicist explains what physics is, he is no longer in physics, but in philosophy. A physiologist who reflects on physiology is philosophizing. If the scientist cannot understand himself as scientist without extrascientific knowledge, how would he explain himself as a human person and the universe as a whole without stepping outside of science? A scientist who pins all certitudes on scientific knowledge implicitly contradicts himself. He has to claim that only those statements which can be demonstrated scientifically are certain. But this claim is self-destructive: it cannot be demonstrated scientifically; therefore it is not certain.

Science is one of the most admirable products of the human mind, but scientism—*corruptio optimi pessima*—is one of its silliest aberrations.

2. Many people deny the existence of God because they feel unable to reconcile the existence of an infinitely powerful and infinitely good God with the prevalence of evil in this world.

We have already struggled with this problem and admitted that philosophy has no satisfactory answer for it, especially as it refers to catastrophic human suffering. There is an answer to the problem, but it is not to be found in philosophy. Philosophy may hint at it, and no philosopher has shown this better than Maurice Blondel in the passages quoted from him above. But these hints are only hints, and they do not, even for those who feel able to take them, cover the whole tragic domain. The answer lies in the prolongation of philosophy: in theology. It supposes that the philosopher—after having explicitly and freely admitted what he cannot not implicitly affirm, that there exists an infinite Being—is willing to listen to this Being as it speaks to him in human history. This willingness will lead him to the stunning spectacle of the Infinite himself assuming not only human flesh but also in this flesh the full brunt of physical evil, to demonstrate in this way that even such evil must have a meaning, must make sense, while yet not to explain totally this meaning or spell out this sense.

All of this goes to show that a complete answer to the problem of evil is not available to the philosopher as philosopher, but only to the philosopher as believer. For the thinkers who are unwilling to make the positive option, to take the momentous step into faith, the problem of evil constitutes a formidable obstacle to an acceptance of God. Natural theology makes full sense only in the light toward which it leads without containing this light in itself. Its full meaning stands revealed only within an attitude of faith.

3. Humanistic atheism is widespread nowadays. It rejects God because he is supposed to interfere with human autonomy and he nullifies the value of human achievements, two main objections which I shall briefly consider.

If the God of whom we have been speaking really exists, people depend totally on him in their activities, in their powers, in their very being. But the modern person is very much aware and proud of his autonomy. One accepts only what one freely chooses to accept. The supreme rule of conduct cannot be imposed from outside; it must come from inside oneself. How then could a person accept a creator, a sovereign being on whom one totally depends and who can, "from outside," impose his will on one, thus to make the human person wholly heteronomous?

Moreover, God, if he exists, not only robs people of their

autonomy but also nullifies all human achievement: he takes away the meaning of human history. Since God is supposed to be the fullness of reality, nothing can be added to him. Everything is precontained in him. He runs the universe and mankind, as he foresees everything which will happen and irresistibly directs the course of history. There is nothing new, nothing unexpected, nothing really important, nothing worth toiling for and eventually dying for. The eons of evolution, the long tragic history of mankind, add absolutely nothing to the fullness of being. If the universe and mankind in it had not existed, it would not make a whit of difference to God. The fullness of reality would be totally unaffected.

These two objections deserve our respect and our sympathy. They derive in great part, however, from a misunderstanding about the relation between God and his creatures. It is true that in the field of human relations the more one depends on another person, the less autonomy one possesses. But things are quite different when we come to our relationship to God. The creature's dependence on him is indeed total. But this total dependence by no means excludes a real autonomy. For God does not simply make or cause his creatures; he makes or causes them to be. He gives them powers and activities that, although they are creatively kept in being by him, are really the powers and the activities of the creatures. The more perfect a creature is, the more these powers and activities come under its own control. In this way we pass gradually from the material activities of minerals to the living activities of plants, to the spontaneous activities of animals, to the free activities of human beings. The nearer it is to God the more autonomous a creature becomes. In the person as person there is total autonomy within total dependence. It is Blondel's great merit to have established so well that human autonomy demands of a person that he freely accept total dependence on God. To reject this dependence is to give up one's autonomy. A freely accepted dependence implies no heteronomy; it coincides with the deepest human yearning.

It is not so easy to answer the other humanistic objection. It is true that for God as theism presents him there can never be anything really new, unexpected, anything which enriches his fullness. That is why the humanist feels attracted to the finite God of Whitehead, who assimilates whatever is new in the universe, to the evolving God of Hegel, who becomes God in and through human history. If one points out to a humanist that a finite or a becoming God is not God, he is ready to give up belief in God.

The best theism can say in this respect is that although for God there never is anything really new, unexpected, enriching, there is, as it were, a displaying of hitherto unrevealed treasures and unexpected beauties. For the universe, for man, these are really new, unexpected; human beings who bring them about are really creative. But it remains true that for God they are not. When hard pressed by the humanist, philosophical theism has to admit that if there had been no creation, no universe, God would be exactly the same as he is now.

That is where panentheism presents certain advantages. Theism is always exposed to the danger of overemphasizing God's transcendence at the expense of his immanence. Panentheism tries to obviate this danger by insisting that the creature is the "otherness" of God, and this otherness of God is *in* God. If the creature is in God, then so are time, evolution, change, history. Then God himself experiences these enriching, novelty-producing processes, not in himself, to be sure, but in his otherness. Thus Karl Rahner can write:

> Christian theology must hold firm to the "immutability" and "eternal" timelessness of God "in himself." At the same time, however, it will have to say that God *himself*, in the otherness of the world, undergoes history, change, and so too time, the time of the world is his own history. As the eternal he does not merely establish time by creating it, but freely assumes it as a specification of his own self. *Assumendo tempus creat tempus*, as we might say, adapting in this a saying of

Augustine's. He thereby causes his own time in order to impart to it his own eternity as the radical effectiveness of his own love. Temporal becoming is not merely the distinguishing characteristic of that which is different from God, but that which, precisely as different from God in this way, and permanently maintaining itself as different, can become, and has become the distinguishing seal of God himself.[2]

It is well understood that the panentheism here endorsed is not quite that of Whitehead, of Hartshorne or of Hegel, although it borrows elements from them. It endorses no *finite* God, no *becoming* God, no God who changes *in himself,* no God who has *essential* reciprocal relations with his creatures, that is, relations which he would need to be really himself. Creatures do not make God relative, but self-relating, relational. They are not the actuation of a potency, but the free overflowing of an infinite actuality.

From what has been explained in the present work we must conclude that (with all due respect to atheists and agnostics) on the unconscious, prereflective level there are no atheists or agnostics. Every human intellect asserts the existence of God as necessarily as every river flows downhill. Man is man only on account of his infinite horizon: a person is an embodied affirmation of the Infinite. He affirms God even in the act by which he tries to deny or to doubt God's existence. The transcendental affirmation of God's existence is an a-priori condition of the possibility of human thinking and action. In itself it is neither reflectively conscious nor free. To establish this has been the aim of the present book. Should this not be true, then we have no case for God in reason.

To become reflectively conscious[3] and to become free, this transcendental affirmation must become categorial: it must be translated into the categories of human thought and language, put into words, welcomed by the will and expressed in action. Man translates it into thought when, having become aware of it, he tries to express it conceptually, when one consciously and freely affirms God as the ultimate end of the movement of the mind. He translates it into action when he lives up to the implications of the reality of the Being he keeps affirming. Practically this means: when he obeys the voice of conscience, when he sincerely acts according to his lights.

The distinctions he makes between the transcendental and the categorial affirmation of God, and the categorial translation of the affirmation both in the intellect and in the will, allow Rahner to distinguish different kinds of atheism.[4]

Some people acknowledge God transcendentally and categorially, both in words and in deeds. Such are the believers who are aware of the divine transcendence and who live up to the knowledge they profess of him. There are other believers who acknowledge God transcendentally, who translate this belief into actions through a good and honest life, but who fail, more or less, to express it correctly in their thinking. The god they consciously profess is an idol; he does not exist as such. But their moral goodness corrects their doctrinal deficiencies. Although the god of their mind may be an idol, the God of their heart is not. There are other believers, or so-called believers, who may or may not have an adequate conception of God, but who do not live up to what God really is. They consciously profess theism, but in reality they are atheists, because they deliberately live as if God did not exist.

Next we have the professed atheists. Some of them are atheists to the fullest extent. They freely reject the transcendental affirmation of God which they are; they reject it not only in thought but also in action. They deny the existence of the real God and make of themselves the center of their universe, in pride, greed and selfishness.

But there are other atheists—Rahner holds that their number keeps increasing—who, in fact, pay some kind of allegiance to the true God. They affirm God's existence transcendentally, as all human beings do; they deny it categorially, in their thinking, but they profess it through their moral activity by being "persons of good will." These are good and unselfish people who cannot accept the existence of God as they understand him. The God of their intelligence is indeed not the real God: he is an idol; he does not exist. They feel unable, mostly on account of their education or of their environment, to proceed intellectually beyond this pseudogod to the mysterious "whereunto" of their intellect and of their will. But they keep groping for him, unconsciously and unfreely on the transcendental level, unconsciously but freely on the categorial level of their moral life. They are not really atheists; Rahner calls them "anonymous theists."

Conclusion[1]

B<small>Y WAY OF CONCLUSION</small> I would like to transcribe, with short comments, a few passages from a great metaphysician, Pierre Scheuer.[2]

> We ask "Why is the affirmation of the divine existence necessary?" and not "Why is the divine existence necessary?" The second question would imply the ontological argument . . . . The question, therefore, is simply: Why do we affirm that there is a first being, and why is that first being *Subsistent Being Itself?*
>
> We answer: In virtue of the principle of identity, understood as a synthetic principle. This principle affirms the adequation of being and the intelligible.[3]

This calls for a few comments. One of Scheuer's basic theses is that the first principle "Whatever is, is" means "Being as it is in itself is identical with being as it is in the itellect."

For modern analysts "Whatever is, is" is a purely analytic principle, a mere tautology. As the basic principle of logic it is indeed nothing more. But it is also the basic principle of metaphysics. As such it is synthetic. That is why Scheuer speaks of the "principle of identity understood as a synthetic principle." There are philosophers who deny that the first principle is synthetic. Such a denial involves a contradiction. As a synthetic principle the principle of identity means "Being in itself is identical with being as it is in the intellect." Try to deny this principle, and in your very denial you affirm it. The principle asserts the identity of being in itself and of being in the intellect. You deny that identity. In your intellect you posit the nonidentity of being in itself and being in the intellect. And you claim that to this nonidentity posited in your intellect corresponds a nonidentity in reality. To some extent you identify reality and your thought of it. Without such an identification it is impossible to deny the synthetic meaning of the first principle. To deny it is to affirm it.

This shows that the human person cannot not make absolute affirmations, such as refer to things in themselves. It is precisely because the human intellect is the faculty of the absolute that it can reach the Absolute. Or rather, the intellect is the faculty of the absolute, because in every affirmation it coaffirms the Absolute.

> This principle affirms the adequation of being and the intelligible. There would be no adequation if the two terms were not equal, if being were not coextensive with the intelligible, and if the intelligible exceeded being. This would be the case if the real were limited, if every reality were composed of act and potency. Such finite, potential objects are intelligible to the extent that they are in act; they equal the intelligible only partially and incompletely, they are not the intelligible. Therefore, the intelligible, or rather that which in the intelligible might exceed the real, would in itself be nothingness: the intelligible would be nonbeing. Hence the affirmation of God is implied in the very principle of thought. To think is to affirm God. To say that one need not rise from finite to the infinite is to say that one need not think.[4]

The reader recognizes our vindication of the principle of intelligibility under another guise. The above passage says in other words that in every one of our existential affirmations the predicate IS is too wide for the subject, and that our intellect yearns for some reality of which it can simply affirm, "This being IS."

If we think at all, we affirm God as objectively existing and as necessary: and this affirmation is infallibly true and requires no other proof beyond itself, because if it were false, the identity between being and the intelligible would likewise be false; hence thought which, by its very essence, is this affirmation would no longer be thought. Suppose that my thought were able to doubt for one instant whether God is: it would be wondering whether it is really the affirmation of such an identity. Still, *even while doubting*, my thought remains such an affirmation. Contradiction would enter into thought.

Why do we affirm God? On the basis of some intuition? No. As the result of some analytic process? No. As the consequence of some process of formal reasoning? Once more, no. Through the process of reasoning we come to understand the nature of thought, and in this way we prove to ourselves that God is the ever-present affirmation; however, this affirmation does not originate in us as the conclusion of an argument. We affirm God in the only way in which he can be affirmed: without any "principle," without intuition, without the ontological argument. Since God has no principle, he cannot be affirmed in virtue of a principle distinct from him. Being is because he is being; hence the sole reason for affirming being is that he is being. And such is indeed the way in which we affirm God. God exists, God is, because he is the intelligible, because he is being.[5]

When Scheuer claims that we do not affirm God because of some intuition, he rejects all intuitive knowledge of God during this life. He does not, however, exclude the possibility that we arrive at the knowledge of God through the intuitive awareness of the movement of our intellect, which is evident from the foregoing paragraph and from the one which follows below. When he says that God is not reached through reasoning, he means that we do not start to affirm his existence at the end of a series of syllogisms. Our reasoning serves only to help us see that we affirm his existence with the very first act of our intellect, even before we start reasoning.

God is affirmed because of the necessary adequation of thought and being; yet this adequation is neither realized nor realizable by the created intellect, for everything which it attains directly is finite, and consequently inadequate. Therefore, *for the created intellect God is that which is required* for this adequation, *that which supplements the deficient intelligibility proper to the finite*. The knowledge of God is identical with the knowledge of the inadequation of the real and the finite; therefore, it is a *negative knowledge*. God is known as that which is beyond the known, as that which remains to be known, as the object of the supreme affirmation, the first principle of all being and of all thought, which remains nevertheless beyond that which is for us the principle of thought. *God is absolutely transcendent*.

Therefore, we should say that we do not know God; he is the Ineffable, the Unknown and the Unknowable. He is not present to knowledge in a positive manner; he remains beyond that which is our object, but he is defined by this very deficiency of our knowledge. We know God through that void which remains in us, through that drive of ours towards the intelligible which, finding only the finite, is almost entirely frustrated; finally as the term of all our activities, although these activities never reach him.[6]

"God is that which supplements the deficient intelligibility proper to the finite." This formula summarizes our vindication of the principle of intelligibility, the backbone of every demonstration of God's existence. We affirm of every reality that it is. But the predicate IS is too wide for every subject. That is why we implicitly add to it a "supplement of intelligibility" by using the principle of intelligibility, as we "exercise" it in our every existential affirmation. Implicitly the affirmation becomes "This being, insofar as it depends on God, is."

We have said that no one can doubt it (the principle of the identity of being and thought), and we have shown the reason why: its denial is unthinkable. Nevertheless, this supreme affirmation remains infinitely mysterious. It constitutes ultimately the very essence of created being, and to fathom it, to perceive its foundation, we would have to fathom our very being and grasp it as it is absolutely. We cannot achieve this, for we remain exterior to ourselves.

Our being is a participation of God: God himself, in some way prolonged and continued outside of himself. Our intellect is a beam of the divine spirit, and our affirmation of God and of being is, in some ineffable manner, the affirmation of God by himself in his creature and by his creature . . . . It is God himself, present in the center of the intellect, according to the very nature of the intellect, hence as intelligible, who moves us, and is the middle term between being and thought.

We can go no further: this presence can neither be perceived nor understood. For God is present in us not as an object of sight but as the principle of sight. He is in us, but in the manner of the eye: the eye of the soul is that which sees; it cannot be seen by itself. Thus we ourselves are a mystery in our own eyes, for we are a divine participation. To understand this participation, we would also have to know the principle of which we participate. And, like our being, our intelligence and our will are unfathomable mysteries. Our intelligence is our light, and, like the sun, it illumines the world of sense; but for itself it is nothing but night and darkness.

Metaphysicians have always put the last touch to their philosophies by denying all forms of thought and of being. Everything sages utter and whatever our gross understanding admires was not worth saying. *The word* is to absolute truth what the being which we are is to the infinite being. . . . We enter real wisdom when we stop speaking. We begin to understand when we are willing not to understand. We cannot give God any name which fits him: he is the one we name by our *silence*.[7]

Notes

Introduction

1. Some philosophers rightly point out that God is not *a* being, but being itself. I shall not discuss this important point here.

2. I use this word in the sense of noncontingent. Many English-speaking philosophers object to this use of the word in this sense; I shall consider their objections later.

3. Langdon Gilkey, *Naming the Whirlwind: The Renewal of God-Language* (Indianapolis: Bobbs-Merrill, 1969).

4. 'Man' here means, of course, *homo sapiens*, not the male of the species.

5. Berger, Peter L., *A Rumor of Angels* (New York: Doubleday, 1969), pp. 52–53.

6. No philosopher has made cleverer use of retortion than Professor Gaston Isaye. About his too little known work read the article of M. X. Moleski, "Retortion: The Method and Metaphysics of Gaston Isaye," *International Philosophical Quarterly* 17 (1977): 59–83.

7. Unless, as some authors do, we mean by intuition any undeniable truth, any truth which one cannot not affirm.

8. L. Malevez, S. J., "Le croyant et le philosophe," in *Pour une théologie de la foi* (Paris: Desclée de Brouwer, 1968), p. 34.

9. The following brief notes about Plato and Aristotle have been taken over from E. de Strycker, *Beknopte Geschiedenis van de antieke Filosofie* (Antwerp, 1967), pp. 112–114, 148–149.

10. Ibid., p. 148.

11. H. Bouillard, S. J., *Connaissance de Dieu* (Paris: Aubier, 1967), p. 88. Bernard Lonergan defends in other words and for other reasons a position which does not differ much from Bouillard's. See his *Philosophy of God and Theology* (Philadelphia: The Westminster Press, 1973), p. x.

12. After having written this, I discovered that Maurice Blondel had used the same comparison.

13. See W. N. Clarke, S. J., "Analytic Philosophy and Language about God," in G. F. McLean, ed., *Christian Philosophy and Religious Renewal* (Washington, D.C.: Catholic University of America Press, 1966), pp. 51–53.

PART ONE: The Existence of God

1. See F. C. Happold, *Mysticism,* pp. 129–142 (shortened references are used for books mentioned in the bibliography).

1. A Posteriori Demonstration of God's Existence

1. Very useful for further study of the topics discussed in this chapter are the following two paperbacks: D. R. Burrill, ed., *The Cosmological Arguments* (Garden City, New York: Doubleday Anchor Books, 1967) and J. Hick, ed., *The Existence of God* (New York: Macmillan, 1964).

2. Thomas Aquinas, *Summa Theologica,* I, q. 2, a. 3.

3. Paul Edwards and Arthur Pap, eds., *A Modern Introduction to Philosophy* (Glencoe, Ill.: The Free Press, 1957), p. 452. It is surprising to see that a generally well-informed philosopher shares a widespread error, when he implies that the supporters of the causal argument hold "the proposition that everything must have a cause *in esse*" (*ibid.*). No scholastic philosopher holds or ever held that proposition. They hold that every *contingent* being has a cause *in esse*. See W. N. Clarke, S. J., "A Curious Blindspot in the Anglo-American Tradition of Antitheistic Argument," *The Monist* 54 (1970): 181–200. See the article of R. Taylor, "Metaphysics and God," in D. Burrill, *The Cosmological Arguments*, pp. 279–295.

4. Typical in this respect is Bertrand Russell's clever quip: "every man has a mother. It does not follow from this that the human race has a mother." For positivists our mother is only an antecedent. I admit that she is also a cause of our beginning. But she is not a cause of our being.

5. Quoted in D. Burrill, *The Cosmological Arguments*, p. 112.

6. I borrow this retortion from G. Isaye, "La finalité de l'intelligence," pp. 61–62.

7. J. Maréchal, *Cahier V*, pp. 583–586. I have quoted this lengthy passage because it is not available in English.

8. The wider sense in which Maréchal interprets the principle of causality is not the usual one.

9. The author prefers not to use the expressions 'principle of sufficient reason' or 'principle of intelligibility' because he considers them ambiguous.

10. Franz Grégoire, *Essai d'une phénoménologie des preuves métaphysiques de Dieu* (Louvain: Editions Universitaires, 1955), p. 79.

11. See the article of R. Taylor, "Metaphysics and God," pp. 279–295.

2. Vindication of God's Existence through the Intellectual Dynamism

1. It will be shown later that the same applies to the human will.

2. L. Wittgenstein, *Tractatus Logico-Philosophicus* 6.45

3. F. Grégoire, *Essai d'une phénoménologie des preuves métaphysiques de Dieu* (Louvain: Editions Universitaires, 1955), p. 111.

4. Ibid., p. 112.

5. (New York: Liberal Arts Press, 1950), p. 22.

6. Very useful for the study of this topic is the following paperback: A. Plantinga, *The Ontological Argument* (Garden City, New York: Doubleday Anchor Books, 1965).

7. St. Anselm, *Proslogion,* quoted by A. Plantinga, *The Ontological Argument*, p. 4. I do not intend to discuss how Anselm himself understood this argument or whether he presented it in several ways. I take it as it is given.

8. Descartes, *Third Meditation,* ibid., p. 32.

9. Ibid., p. 38.

10. Ibid., pp. 41–42.

11. Ibid., p. 43.

12. Leibniz, *The New Essays Concerning Human Understanding,* ibid., p. 55.

13. I use the simple form as presented in *The Monist*, vol. 54, no. 2 (1970), under the title "On Proofs for the Existence of God" and as reprinted in John Donnelly, *Logical Analysis and Contemporary Theism*, p. 7. A more elaborated presentation may be found in J. F. Ross, *Philosophical Theology,* chapter 3.

14. Ross, "On Proofs for the Existence of God," p. 14.

15. Kant admitted that the human mind cannot help having an idea of God. The "transcendental illusion" is unavoidable.

16. From *The Critique of Pure Reason,* trans. by Norman K. Smith, quoted by Plantinga, *The Ontological Argument*, p. 59.

17. Ibid.

18. Ibid., p. 61–62.

19. J. Maréchal, *Le point de départ de la métaphysique,* cahier III, *La critique de Kant* (Brussels: L'Edition Universelle, 1944), pp. 259–262.

20. Kant, *Critique of Pure Reason,* A 586–587; B 614–615.

21. J. Maréchal, *Cahier III*, p. 259.

22. See Donceel, *A Maréchal Reader*, pp. 117–189; 244–250.

23. See his *Spirit in the World*, pp. 135–145. Also Anita Röper, *The Anonymous Christian* (New York: Sheed & Ward, 1966), chapter three.

24. W. Richardson, S. J., *Heidegger: Through Phenomenology to Thought* (The Hague: Martinus Nijhoff, 1963), p. 474. I thank Professor Richardson for his useful suggestions.

25. A. Flew and A. MacIntyre, *New Essays in Philosophical Theology*, p. 106.

26. Ibid., p. 99.

27. Quoted in A. Plantinga, *The Ontological Argument*, p. 119.

28. Flew and MacIntyre, *New Essays in Philosophical Theology*, p. 114.

29. This is taken over from G. Isaye, "La finalité de l'intelligence," pp. 91–92.

3. Blondel's Demonstration of the Existence of God

1. M. Blondel's main work is *L'Action: Essai d'une critique de la vie et d'une science de la pratique*. Paris, Alcan, 1893. Reissued by Presses Universitaires de France, 1950. This work has not been translated into English. But a good condensation-translation with an instructive preface and comments has been published by J. M. Somerville under the title, *Total Commitment: Blondel's L'Action* (Washington: Corpus Books, 1968) (Available from Philosophical Exchange, Box 11144, Bethabera, Winston-Salem, N.C., 27040). Very useful for those who intend to study Blondel's work is H. Bouillard, *Blondel et le Christianisme* (Paris: Seuil, 1961). English translation by J. M. Somerville, *Blondel and Christianity*, (Washington: Corpus Books, 1969).

Because most of Blondel's writings are not available in English translation, I shall not hesitate to quote him abundantly in my own translation.

2. I call "dogmatic empiricists" those philosophers who claim that all our knowledge comes from the senses and who, nevertheless, construct a metaphysics that contains absolutely certain truths.

3. S. Strasser, *The Soul in Metaphysical and Empirical Psychology* (Pittsburgh: Duquesne University Press, 1957). See J. Donceel, *Philosophical Anthropology*, (New York: Sheed and Ward, 1967), chapter one.

4. See Donceel, *Maréchal Reader*, pp. 163–171.

5. See *Etudes blondéliennes*, I, pp. 82–83; quoted by H. Bouillard, *Blondel and Christianity*, p. 10.

6. M. Blondel, *L'Action*, p. xxi.

7. Ibid., pp. 406–407.

8. Ibid., pp. 343–344.

9. Ibid., pp. 346–347.

10. Ibid., p. 348.

11. Ibid., p. 354–355.

12. "L'Illusion idéaliste" in *Premiers écrits,* II, p. 116; quoted by H. Bouillard, *Blondel and Christianity,* p. 185.

13. Ibid., p. 117; in Bouillard, *Blondel and Christianity,* p. 185.

14. Blondel, *L'Action,* p. 426.

15. Ibid., pp. 351–352.

16. Ibid., p. 374.

17. Ibid., p. 382.

18. Ibid., p. 383. Blondel gives us here a valuable hint for a partial solution of the problem of evil. See also pages 397–400. Blondel himself lived in blindness the last 23 years of his life.

4. Knowledge of God and the Supernatural

1. Does such a topic belong in a book on philosophy? For a remarkable answer to this question read Maurice Blondel, *The Letter on Apologetics,* trans. A. Dru and I. Trethowan (New York: Holt, Rinehart & Winston, 1964).

2. Aristotle, *Nicomachean Ethics,* bk. 10, ch. 7. From R. McKeon, ed. *Introduction to Aristotle* (New York: The Modern Library, 1947), pp. 533–534.

3. This is the main theme of K. Rahner's book *Hearers of the Word*. See G. A. McCool, ed., *A Rahner Reader,* chapters one to three.

4. Blondel, *L'Action,* p. 437.

5. Ibid., p. 428.

6. J. F. Ross, *Philosophical Theology,* pp. 15–16.

7. "I do not think that in this life people arrive at natural knowledge of God without God's grace, but what I do not doubt is that the knowledge they so attain is natural." B. Lonergan, "Natural Knowledge of God," in *A Second Collection,* ed. W. F. J. Ryan, S. J., and B. J. Tyrrell, S. J. (Philadelphia: Westminster Press, 1974), p. 133.

8. M. Blondel, *La pensée,* vol. II (Paris: Alcan, 1934), p. 370.

9. Blondel, *L'Action,* p. 442 (my emphasis).

5. Can God's Existence Be Demonstrated Scientifically?

1. G. Isaye, S. J., "La métaphysique des simples," *Nouvelle Revue Théologique* 92 (1960): 691–692.

2. Other thinkers such as M. Polanyi favor this trend.

3. See J. Donceel, "Teilhard: Scientist or Philosopher?" *International Philosophical Quarterly* 5 (1965): 248–266. Also G. Isaye, "The Method of Teilhard," *The New Scholasticism* 41 (1967): 31–57.

PART TWO: The Essence of God

1. Henri Bergson, *The Two Sources of Morality and Religion* (1935; reprint ed., Notre Dame: University of Notre Dame Press, 1977), p. 262.

2. See Maréchal, *Cahier V,* pp. 345–346. Also idem, *Le point de départ de la métaphysique,* cahier I, *De l'ântiquité à la fin du Moyen Age* (Louvain, 1927²), pp. 90–93.

3. J. Defever, *La preuve réelle de Dieu,* p. 78.

6. God's Nature according to Traditional Philosophy

1. *Summa Theologica,* I, q. 19, a. 2, c.

2. J. Maréchal, *Le point de départ de la métaphysique,* cahier IV, *Le système idéaliste chez Kant et les postkantiens* (Brussels: L'Edition Universelle, 1947), pp. 434–435.

3. Georg Hegel, *Lectures on the Philosophy of Religion,* trans. by E. B. Spiers and J. B. Sanderson (London: Kegan Paul, Trench, Trubner and Company, 1895), I, pp. 30–31.

4. H. Glockner's *Jubileumausgabe der Werke Hegels* (Stuttgart: F. Frommann, 1949 ff.), XVIII, p. 253.

5. M. Blondel, *L'Être et les êtres* (Paris: Presses Universitaires de France, 1935), p. 193.

6. Ibid., p. 520.

7. Among the many books worth reading on this topic let the following be mentioned: Langdon Gilkey, *Maker of Heaven and Earth* (Garden City, New York: Doubleday Anchor Books, 1965); Olivier Rabut, *God in an Evolving Universe* (New York: Herder and Herder, 1966); and Piet Schoonenberg, *God's World in the Making* (Pittsburgh: Duquesne University Press, 1964).

8. P. Teilhard de Chardin, *Oeuvres,* vol. X (Paris: Seuil, 1969), pp. 27–32.

9. K. Rahner, *Hominisation* (New York: Herder & Herder, 1965), p. 80.

10. Hence admitting that God creates both freely and necessarily, out of love, does not contradict the decree of the First Vatican Council. See *Ds* 3025, *Dz* 1805.

11. This rather primitive mentality subsists in people who, when visited by adversity, complain and wonder, "Why did God do this to me?"

12. A categorial cause is one that operates on the level of the categories, in space and time, hence on the same level as its effects.

13. "Somewhat" I am not asserting that God is the formal cause of these events.

14. See Béla Weismahr, *Gottes Wirken in der Welt* (Frankfurt: Knecht, 1973).

15. See his *Introduction to the Philosophy of Religion* (London: Macmillan, 1969), pp. 139–140. I do not claim that this comparison fits the case perfectly.

16. This is a frequently recurring theme of K. Rahner's theology.

17. See P. Schoonenberg, S. J., "God or Man: A False Dilemma," in *The Christ* (New York: Herder & Herder, 1971), pp. 13–32.

18. Karl Rahner no longer seems to accept this traditional explanation. He writes: "Should we not honestly call 'to will' the 'allowing' of something which one might prevent without infringing upon the freedom of this action? God can will the radical evil of sin in and with a finite world." *Theological Investigations*, vol. XIII [London: Darton, Longman and Todd), p. 141.

19. John Hick, *Evil and the God of Love* (London: Fontana Library, 1975), pp. 302–311. The book combines theological and philosophical considerations.

20. Ibid., p. 311.

21. P. Teilhard de Chardin, *How I Believe* (New York: Harper & Row, 1969), p. 89.

22. *Oeuvres*, vol. XI (Paris: Seuil, 1973), pp. 211–212.

23. Blondel, *L'Action*, pp. 380–384.

24. "It is possible that there is or will be in this world something, say a kingdom of heaven, of so great value that any world without it would be worse than this one and that further the present evil is a logically necessary condition of it" (John Wisdom, "God and Evil," *Mind* 44 (1935): 4; quoted by J. Hick, *Evil and the God of Love*, p. 309.

25. Blondel, *L'Action*, p. 395. For a somewhat similar treatment of the problem see J. Hick, *Evil and the God of Love*, pp. 293ff.

7. The Essence of God according to Modern Philosophies

1. For a clear and short exposition of the panentheism of C. Hartshorne see the introduction of C. Hartshorne and W. T. Reese, *Philosophers Speak of God* (Chicago: University of Chicago Press, 1953), pp. 1–25. See also Walter Stokes, S. J., "God for Today and Tomorrow," in D. Brown, R. E. James Jr. and G. Reeves, *Process Philosophy and Christian Thought* (New York: Bobbs-Merrill, 1971), pp. 244–263. There is a good short entry on *Panentheism* by E. R. Naughton in the *New Catholic Encyclopedia*.

2. C. Hartshorne, *The Divine Relativity* (New Haven: Yale University Press, 1948), p. 90.

3. For Hartshorne (and also for Hegel) creation might be called *constitutive* of God. I would rather call it *consecutive* upon God.

4. Gómez Caffarena, *Metafísica trascendental,* p. 317.

5. M. Blondel, *La pensée* (Paris: Presses universitaires de France, 1948), p. 421.

6. "This doctrine of the 'immanence' of the world in God is false and heretical only if it denies creation and the distinction of the world from God (and not only of God from the world) (*Dz.* 1782)."

7. K. Rahner and H. Vorgrimler, *Theological Dictionary* (New York: Herder & Herder, 1965), pp. 333–334 (translation slightly corrected).

8. M. Blondel, *L'Être et les êtres* (Paris: Alcan, 1935), p. 206.

9. Blondel's note to *Semetipsum exinanivit* (He has emptied himself):
Needless to say that while we make use of a metaphor taken from St. Paul, we intend neither to usurp on behalf of philosophical theses the Apostle's authority nor to take literally a simple comparison. Such an image is useful in order to counterbalance the influence of the opposite and usual image, which is no less deficient than the one we use here. There is no void outside of God anymore than there is one in him. But by evoking the memory of the infinite condescendence and humility of God in behalf of his creature, we may perhaps better understand the creative design than by suggesting the image of a quasi-physical and preexisting void that would have to be filled rather than to have to be mercifully hollowed out by the Creator. But once more let us not be deceived by the literal meaning of the metaphors.

10. Blondel, *L'Être et les êtres,* pp. 206–209.

11. Ibid., p. 311.

12. Dupré, *The Other Dimension,* p. 389.

13. This is a basic idea of Hegel's philosophy.

14. Dupré, *The Other Dimension,* p. 389.

15. For a clear, although contested, introduction to Hegel's thought see W. T. Stace, *The Philosophy of Hegel,* (New York: Dover Publications, 1955). Excellent things about God in Hegel's system are found in Emil L. Fackenheim, *The Religious Dimension in Hegel's Thought* (Bloomington, Ind.: Indiana University Press, 1967) and also in Quentin Lauer, "Hegel on Proofs of God's Existence," *Kant-Studien 55* (1964): 443–465.

16. J. Maréchal, *Studies in the Psychology of the Mystics* (Albany, N.Y.: Magi Books, 1964), p. 299.

17. K. Barth, *Die protestantische Theologie im 19 Jahrhundert* (Zollikon/Zürich: Evangelischer Verlag, 1952), p. 378, quoted by H. Küng, *Menschwerdung Gottes* (Freiburg: Herder, 1970), p. 556.

18. G. Hegel, *System der Philosophie*, part III (Glockner X) (Stuttgart: Frommann, 1958), p. 454.

19. G. Hegel, *Begriff der Religion*, ed. by G. Lasson (Hamburg: Meiner, 1966), pp. 146 and p. 148, emphasis by Hegel.

20. Ibid., p. 257.

21. Hegel, *System der Philosophie* (Glockner, X), p. 454. My emphasis.

22. See, for instance, Quentin Lauer, "Hegel's Pantheism," *Thought* 54 (1979): 5–23.

23. Franz Grégoire, *Études hégéliennes* (Louvain: Editions Universitaires, 1958), p. 211–212.

24. Ibid., pp. 205–206.

25. H. Rondet, *Hégélianisme et Christianisme* (Paris: Lethielleux, 1965), p. 71.

26. E. Fackenheim, *The Religious Dimension*, p. 193.

27. Ibid., pp. 200–201.

28. Ibid., p. 201.

29. Ibid., p. 191.

30. Ibid., p. 197.

31. Thus, for Hegel the neoplatonic philosophy had already discovered the mystery of the preworldly Trinity.

32. E. Fackenheim, *The Religious Dimension*, p. 167.

33. Ibid., p. 127.

34. Ibid., p. 193.

35. See ibid., p. 155.

36. *Philosophie der Religion* (Glockner II), p. 496.

37. Lauer, "Hegel on Proofs of God's Existence," p. 448.

38. Donceel, *Maréchal Reader*, p. 225.

39. Franz Grégoire, *Études hégéliennes* (Louvain: Editions Universitaires, 1958), p. 124.

40. E. Coreth, *Metaphysik* (Innsbruck: Tyrolia, 1964²), p. 91; idem, *Metaphysics*, pp. 50–51.

41. Coreth, *Metaphysik*, pp. 92–93; idem, *Metaphysics*, pp. 51–52.

42. K. Rahner, *Theological Investigations*, vol. IV, trans. by Kevin Smyth (Baltimore: Helicon, 1966), pp. 113–114.

43. Ibid., vol. XI (New York: Seabury Press, 1974), pp. 307–308.

44. Hans Küng, *Menschwerdung Gottes* (Freiburg: Herder, 1970), P. 556.

45. Ibid., p. 551.

46. G. Hegel, *Science of Logic*, trans. by A. V. Miller (New York: Humanities Press, 1969), pp. 143–144.

47. J. Gómez Caffarena, *Metafísica trascendental* (Madrid: Revista de Occidente, 1970), p. 114.

48. Gregoire, *Études hégéliennes,* p. 23.

49. Karl Rahner, *Grundkurs des Glaubens* (Freiburg: Herder, 1976), pp. 71–72.

50. Ibid., p. 72.

51. That may be why Aquinas is not afraid of saying that God "works throughout all activity after the manner of all these three causes, final, efficient and *formal*" (*Summa Theologica*, I, q. 105, a. 5). (My emphasis).

52. Gómez Caffarena, *Metafísica trascendental,* p. 205.

8. Atheism

1. Among the many books worth reading on this topic a very readable one is I. Lepp, *Atheism in Our Time* (New York: Macmillan, 1963).

2. *Theological Investigations,* vol. XI (New York: Seabury Press, 1974), p. 308.

3. There are many things in our life which we "live" but to which we never give thought. They are conscious, but it takes some attention and effort to make them reflectively conscious.

4. K. Rahner, "Atheism and Implicit Christianity," *Theology Digest* (Feb. 1968): 43–56. What follows is a condensation of this paper.

Conclusion

1. This conclusion has been taken over, with a few minor modifications, from J. Donceel, *Natural Theology* (New York: Sheed & Ward, 1962), pp. 165–171.

2. The whole text has been made available by Daniel J. Shine, S. J., in his *An Interior Metaphysics* (Weston, Mass.: Weston College Press, 1966). Maréchal writes about the first principle in *Le Thomisme,* pp. 561–568. Donceel, *Maréchal Reader,* pp. 228–231.

3. Pierre Scheuer, "Deux textes inédits," *Nouvelle Revue Théologique* 79 (1957): 823; Shine, *An Interior Metaphysics*, p. 162.

4. Scheuer, "Deux textes inédits," p. 823; Shine, *An Interior Metaphysics,* pp. 162–163.

5. Scheuer, "Deux textes inédits," p. 824; Shine, *An Interior Metaphysics,* pp. 163–164.

6. Scheuer, "Deux textes inédits," pp. 825–826; Shine, *An Interior Metaphysics,* pp. 167–168.

7. Scheuer, "Deux textes inédits," pp. 826–827; Shine, *An Interior Metaphysics,* pp. 169–171.

Bibliography

THE PURPOSE of the following bibliography is to mention, not all the books which would deserve to be read, but only some of those which might be most useful for those who desire to deepen the study of the problem of God along the lines suggested in this work.

The main work is and remains

J. Maréchal. *Le point de départ de la métaphysique*. Cahier V, *Le Thomisme devant la philosophie critique*. Brussels: L'Edition Universelle, 1949.

A summary in English of this book, with extracts:

J. Donceel, ed. *A Maréchal Reader*. New York: Herder & Herder, 1970.

A. Grégoire. *Immanence et transcendance*. Brussels: L'Edition Universelle, 1939.

J. Defever. *La preuve réelle de Dieu*. Brussels: L'Edition Universelle, 1953.

L. Malevez. *Transcendance de Dieu et création des valeurs*. Paris: Desclée de Brouwer, 1958.

G. Isaye. "La finalité de l'intelligence et l'objection kantienne." *Revue Philosophique de Louvain* 51 (1953): 42–100 (highly recommended to all who wish to understand the thought of Maréchal).

D. J. Shine, ed. *An Interior Metaphysics: The Philosophical Synthesis of Pierre Scheuer, S.J.* Weston (Mass.): Weston College Press, 1966.

225

O. Muck. *The Transcendental Method*. Trans. by W. D. Seidensticker. New York: Herder & Herder, 1968.

H. de Lubac. *The Discovery of God*. Trans. by A. Dru. New York: Kenedy, 1960.

K. Rahner. *Spirit in the World*. Trans. by W. Dych, S. J. New York: Herder & Herder, 1968.

_____. *Hearers of the Word*. Trans. by M. Richards. New York: Herder & Herder, 1969.

Large extracts from the translation of the easier-to-understand original first edition are in:

G. A. McCool, ed. *A Rahner Reader*, pp. 1–65. New York: Herder & Herder, 1975.

B. J. F. Lonergan. *Philosophy of God and Theology*. Philadelphia: Westminster Press, 1973.

José Gómez Caffarena. *Metafísica trascendental*. Madrid: Revista de Occidente, 1970.

E. Coreth. *Metaphysik*. Innsbruck: Tyrolia, 1964.

English abbreviated edition by J. Donceel, with a critique by B. Lonergan:

E. Coreth. *Metaphysics*. New York: Herder & Herder, 1968.

Johannes B. Lotz. *Transzendentale Erfahrung*. Freiburg: Herder, 1978.

For a phenomenology and philosophy of religion:

L. Dupré. *The Other Dimension*. Garden City, N.Y.: Doubleday, 1972.

J. Donceel, review of *The Other Dimension*, by L. Dupré, *International Philosophical Quarterly* 15 (1975): 99–109.

A good introduction to the modern problem of God:

E. M. Tyrrell. *Man: Believer and Unbeliever*, chapters 1 to 4. New York: Alba House, 1973.

A solid historical study:

J. Collins. *God in Modern Philosophy*. Chicago: Regnery, 1959.

On different conceptions of God:

H. P. Owen. *Concepts of Deity*. New York: Herder & Herder, 1971.

On some of the modern problems in the field:

A. Flew and A. MacIntyre. *New Essays in Philosophical Theology*. New York: Macmillan, 1964.

Also,

J. Donnelly, ed. *Logical Analysis and Contemporary Theism*. New York: Fordham University Press, 1972.

A philosophy of God within the framework of analytic philosophy:

J. F. Ross. *Philosophical Theology*. Indianapolis: Bobbs-Merrill, 1969.

Or shorter, easier treatment:

J. F. Ross. *Introduction to the Philosophy of Religion*. New York: Macmillan, 1969.

On the mystical approach to God:

J. Maréchal. *Studies in the Psychology of the Mystics*. Albany, N.Y.: Magi Books, 1964.

E. O'Brien. *Varieties of Mystic Experience*. New York: Mentor-Omega Books, 1964.

F. C. Happold. *Mysticism: A Study and an Anthology*. Baltimore: Penguin Books, 1958.

The case against God:

P. Angeles, ed. *Critiques of God*. Buffalo, N.Y.: Prometheus Books, 1976.

Index

228